LIVING ZEN

LIVING ZEN

A PRACTICAL GUIDE TO A
BALANCED EXISTENCE

SETH ZUIHŌ SEGALL, PhD

ROCKRIDGE
PRESS

Interior and Cover Designer: Erik Jacobsen
Photo Art Director/Art Manager: Samantha Ulban
Editor: Shannon Criss
Production Editor: Ashley Polikoff
Stocksy/Mem Studio, Cover, Amanda Leon, p.12. All other images used under license © iStock. Author Photo courtesy of Sue Mirialakis.

ISBN: Print 978-1-64611-583-9 | eBook 978-1-64611-584-6
R0

*To my grandchildren, may you live happy,
fulfilling, and virtuous lives.*

Contents

Introduction

We all want to live the best lives we possibly can. For a lot of us, this means achieving happiness and developing a sense of inner peace. But it could also mean obtaining personal and professional success, nurturing good relationships, and, ultimately, doing right by others. Despite the fact we may all have similar goals, most of us encounter difficulties along the way. Let's face it: Life is hard, we're pretty much imperfect, and sometimes we could use a little help along the way. Zen offers the kind of help we seek.

I began my own Buddhist practice a quarter century ago. As a clinical psychologist, I often saw chronic pain patients who weren't helped by traditional methods, and that's how I first became interested in meditation as a treatment for pain and suffering. The more I learned about meditation, however, the more I realized it wasn't just something to offer my patients. It was something for me, too.

The first fifteen years of my practice wasn't in Zen, but in the vipassana (insight meditation) tradition of Theravada Buddhism. I've practiced Zen for the last decade and eventually ordained as a Zen priest as part of my path of study and service. My role as a Zen priest has enabled me to officiate at rites of passage, provide pastoral care in my local hospital, and engage in interfaith dialogue with clergy from other religions. It has also provided unique opportunities for deepening my own practice. My 25 years of vipassana and Zen practice has strengthened my ability to be more fully and intimately present, to be at home in my body, to accept life's circumstances with equanimity, and to focus on the well-being of others. It has also given me an inner calm I can retain in almost all circumstances.

Zen can be thought of as a set of principles and practices. It can also be thought of as a philosophy, religion, path, or way of life. It doesn't fit neatly into any one category. More than being a set of beliefs, however, Zen is something one engages in and does. It's the way we meditate, deal skillfully with our thoughts and emotions, and engage in our relationships with friends, coworkers, family, and passersby. It's the spirit we put into the way we do the laundry, wash the dishes, change the diapers, and earn a paycheck. It encompasses every aspect of our lives. Even if one has no interest in "becoming a Buddhist," it offers practical wisdom about life that anyone can benefit from.

Although fully understanding Zen requires decades of devoted practice, Zen has a great deal to offer the beginner, too. It helps us reduce our suffering and develop inner calm. It helps us pay attention to our lives in fresh new ways and see the world from a different perspective. It gives us tools to change how we think about the things that bother us and how to connect more fully with others in authentic, effective, and meaningful ways. It helps us appreciate those things that are going right in our lives as well as accept those difficulties we can't change. It promises a life that is vibrant, alive, and in harmony with the universe. If you would like this kind of help, this book is an introduction to using Zen insights to better your life. Part 1 of this book will introduce you to what Zen is, part 2 will show you how to use Zen wisdom in your daily life, and part 3 will offer suggestions and resources for delving more deeply into a Zen practice.

May this book give you the tools to attain a deeper sense of happiness and well-being.

PART ONE

ZEN 101

Before learning how to employ Zen teachings in your daily life, you will first need to learn some Zen basics: its origin, what it teaches, and how to put it into practice. Chapter 1 gives a short account of Zen's relationship to Buddhism, then chapter 2 introduces core Zen concepts and practices.

Chapter One

THE ZEN ORIGIN

This chapter introduces the origins and basic teachings of Buddhism and Zen. You will learn about the history of Buddhism in India, China, and Japan, and Zen's place in that history. You will also learn about basic Buddhist philosophy, the rise of Mahayana Buddhism in India, China, and Japan, and what makes Zen distinctive. Finally, you will be introduced to modern Zen practice, what Zen practitioners do, and what they hope to accomplish.

The History of Buddhism

According to legend, a young Indian prince named Siddhartha Gautama, who lived around the fifth century BCE, left his father's palace to seek an answer to the problem of suffering. After six long years of meditation and fasting, he was no closer to his goal. One day he sat beneath a fig tree vowing to meditate until he found what he was seeking. Forty-nine days into his meditation, he attained Enlightenment and became known as "the **Buddha**," which means "the Awakened One." Over the next 40 years, he traveled throughout India, teaching an end to suffering and the path to inner peace.

WHAT DID THE BUDDHA TEACH?

SUFFERING IS AN INEVITABLE PART OF LIFE. We all suffer in great and small ways, from intense pain and grief to mild disappointment and vague dissatisfaction. The Buddha taught that we make suffering worse by trying to hold on to pleasures that can't last, or by resisting unpleasant things we can't do anything about. We're happier when we allow our pleasant and unpleasant feelings to come and go, accepting things as they are. He also taught that our belief that we are permanent, unchanging "selves" is another cause of suffering. We must accept that we, like everything else, are subject to change.

KARMA, OR CAUSE-AND-EFFECT, IS ANOTHER KEY BUDDHIST TEACHING. The Law of **Karma** states that what we think and do now determines who we will become in the future. If we engage in angry thoughts and actions, we become angry people. If we engage in kind thoughts and actions, we become kind people. We have the power to become the people we wish to be.

THE BUDDHA ALSO OUTLINED THE PATH TO THE END OF SUFFERING. He taught that we could obtain inner peace by acting ethically, training our minds through meditation, and understanding the truths of karma, the causes of suffering, the nature of impermanence, and our false ideas about ourselves.

THE BUDDHA TAUGHT THAT WE ARE REBORN AFTER DEATH IN ACCORDANCE WITH OUR KARMA. We can be reborn into a hell or heaven, or as ghosts, animals, humans, or demigods depending on how we've lived our lives. When we become Enlightened, we put an end to the endless cycle of rebirth and dwell in the peace of *Nirvana*. While many Buddhists believe in the reality of rebirth, many others believe that rebirth is a metaphor for how our current thoughts and actions create a heaven or hell for us in our one and only life.

BRANCHES OF BUDDHISM

There are three main branches of Buddhism: *Theravada* (the Buddhism of Sri Lanka, Myanmar, Malaysia, Laos, and Cambodia), *Mahayana* (the Buddhism of China, Japan, Korea, and Vietnam), and *Vajrayana* (the Buddhism of Tibet, Nepal, Bhutan, Mongolia, and Siberia). *Zen* is a type of Mahayana Buddhism that originated in China in 400 to 500 CE, and then spread to Japan, Korea, and Vietnam. It emphasizes meditation as the path to Enlightenment.

Mahayana Buddhism

Mahayana Buddhism began between 100 BCE and 200 CE in ancient India. The word "Mahayana" means "great vehicle," because Mahayana Buddhists vow to bring all sentient beings to

Enlightenment rather than just pursuing their own personal Nirvana. Mahayana Buddhism teaches that everyone has "**Buddha-Nature**," or the basic capacity for Enlightenment.

Mahayana Buddhism also stresses that nothing exists in, of, and by itself; things only exist in their interrelatedness with everything else. You, for example, wouldn't be "you" if it weren't for your parents; the society and culture you were born into; enough food, water, air, and sunlight; a habitable planet the correct distance from the sun; a universe that obeys the laws of physics, and so on. You are interdependent with the vast web of existence, and so is everything else. Buddhism uses the term "emptiness" to describe this interdependence, because all things are said to be empty of "self-existence."

The Rise of Zen Buddhism

According to legend, Zen began in the fifth or sixth century CE, when an Indian teacher named **Bodhidharma** traveled to China. Before Bodhidharma's arrival, Chinese Buddhism emphasized studying translations of Indian Buddhist texts, establishing temples and monasteries, engaging in devotional practices, and conducting rituals. Bodhidharma introduced a new form of Mahayana Buddhism that relied on meditation rather than on speculative philosophy or rituals. The Chinese named this new form *Chan*. When Chan appeared in Japan in the twelfth century, the Japanese called it Zen. Both words are derived from *dhyana*, the Sanskrit word for meditation.

Zen teachings were strongly influenced by Taoist philosophy, which was a feature of Chinese culture before Buddhism's arrival. Taoism teaches the Way of Nature: the wise person lives in accordance with the natural order of things. Taoism added qualities of spontaneity, naturalness, and simplicity to Zen.

There are many famous Zen masters who helped develop and clarify original Zen teachings. Among the most prominent was the thirteenth century Japanese Zen Master Eihei Dogen who founded the **Soto** School of Japanese Zen that emphasizes **shikantaza** or "just sitting." Another pioneer was the seventeenth to eighteenth century Japanese Zen Master Hakuin Ekaku, who reinvigorated the **Rinzai** School of Japanese Zen and reorganized **koan** study.

The Enso: A Symbol of Zen

An **enso** is a hand-drawn circle, executed in a single ink brushstroke, that fully expresses the artist's state of being in the moment. The enso, like Zen itself, is notable for its naturalness, spontaneity, and simplicity. It can variously express wholeness, emptiness, perfection, and Enlightenment. Enlightenment is sometimes compared to the moon at night or a great round mirror, both circular images of illumination and clarity.

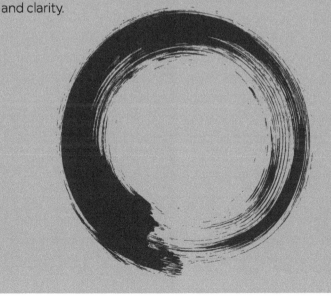

Present-Day Zen

While Zen is an ancient and ongoing tradition in China, Japan, Korea, and Vietnam, it spread throughout the West during the twentieth and twenty-first centuries. The first Westerners interested in Zen were mostly scholars, artists, writers, poets, and psychoanalysts who believed Zen offered important insights into well-being, spirituality, and creativity. Today, it's of interest to people of various backgrounds and belief systems, and not always in the context of traditional practice. People commonly use the word "zen" to refer to feelings of peace, tranquility, and "being in the zone." Advertisers use it, hoping its associations with "being chill" will sell products. While colloquial and commercial references to Zen have become part of our culture, they have little to do with what real Zen has to offer serious practitioners.

Western Zen practitioners meet in sitting groups, *zendos*, temples, and retreat centers. Their practice primarily consists of sitting (**zazen**), walking (**kinhin**), and **koan** meditations; chanting; studying the Zen ethical precepts; listening to teacher talks (**teisho**); and meeting individually with teachers (**daisan *or* dokusan**) to work on *koans* or discuss their progress on the Zen path. Practitioners also go on multiday silent meditation retreats (**sesshin**) in which they meditate for many hours over the course of each day.

Many practitioners continue to remain adherents of their original faiths. They practice not to become Buddhists, but to use Zen wisdom in their daily lives. They hope to gain a sense of inner peace, to approach life in a more positive way, and to gain balance and perspective in dealing with difficulties.

Many practitioners also hope to experience meditative states in which they directly feel the interrelatedness of everything (**satori** or **kensho**.) Zen teaches that while our everyday perception is of a world made up of separate, discrete objects—at the deepest level, things exist as part of a vast ever-changing field of interrelatedness. Zen goes one step further and teaches that these two ways of seeing the world—as separate and as interrelated—are ultimately the same. Zen calls this unity of oneness and many-ness "non-duality," which can only be directly grasped and appreciated through meditative experience. "Non-dual" experiences offer new perspectives that change how we understand ourselves and the world and allow us to live more peaceful and balanced lives.

Chapter Two

TO BE ZEN

Now that you know Zen's background and history, it's time to introduce the basics of Zen practice. Zen uses a variety of meditation techniques, including sitting, walking, and chanting meditations. All meditations have the same purpose: to teach us how to be wholeheartedly and undividedly present in the moment, instead of our usual mode of being lost in thoughts and imaginings. We approach these meditations with a "beginner's mind"—meaning freshly, without preconceptions and expectations. Zen isn't only about meditation, however. It's also about developing qualities of the heart: compassion and kindness. Zen is grounded in the intention to reduce suffering—not just our own, but everyone's.

The Zen Practice

Zen practice involves cultivating inner stillness, listening deeply to the present moment, and realizing one's interconnection with all things. It also entails learning how to focus one's attention, and to refocus it again and again whenever it has strayed. The following Zen practices will help you develop these abilities and enrich your life.

ZAZEN

Zazen, or seated meditation, is the quintessential Zen practice. There are three types of zazen: breath-focused meditation, shikan-taza, and koan meditation. To do zazen, assume an open, upright sitting posture (see illustration). However you sit—on a cushion, bench, or chair—your ears, shoulders, and hips should be aligned, your chin slightly tucked, and your eyes partly closed and looking downward in front of you. Place your left hand atop your right hand, palms up, with your thumbs gently touching. If you're on a cushion, both knees should touch the floor, so that your rear end and knees

Half-Lotus

Burmese

form a tripod supporting your body. Your abdomen should be able to expand and contract freely with your breath.

You may sit zazen in a full lotus or half lotus position, or in the Burmese style, using a meditation cushion (**zafu**) and mat (**zabuton**). If your body isn't flexible enough, the Burmese position might be more comfortable. You can also kneel Japanese style using a *seiza* bench for support or sit in a chair. When using a chair, be sure to sit upright and avoid slumping. Your feet should also touch the floor.

BREATH-FOCUSED MEDITATION

Most Zen beginners start zazen with breath-focused meditation. To do this, focus all your attention on the physical sensations of breathing in your abdomen, as you breathe in and out normally. You may find it hard to keep your attention focused; after a few breaths your mind will probably drift off into distractions. Each time this happens, try to catch your mind as soon as it drifts off, and gently return it to your breathing. Count your breaths to keep your mind focused. Count to ten, then start over again. If you lose count, begin again with "one." Breath-focused meditation is about training your mind to stay focused and grounded in the present moment.

SHIKANTAZA

Shikantaza means "just sitting." In shikantaza, you keep your mind steady and focused on the passing parade of transient sensations and mental states. Do this without attaching to them or pushing them away, allowing sensations, thoughts, and feelings to come and go like clouds floating across the blue sky. The mind acts like a clear, still mirror reflecting everything without comment. In shikantaza, our only goal is being present in a vast field of acceptance.

KOANS

Koans are puzzling questions, statements, or snippets of brief dialogue between ancient Zen masters and their students, that serve as a focus of meditation. "What is the sound of one hand clapping?" and "Show me your original face before your mother and father were born" are famous koans. Zen students meet regularly with a teacher to attempt to demonstrate their understanding of a koan. Koans cannot be logically "solved" and have no set pat "answers." It may take weeks, months, or years before a student responds in a way that adequately expresses his or her authentic realization of Zen.

Mu

"Joshu's Dog" is often the first koan Zen students work on. The koan states, "A monk asked Zen Master Joshu, 'Does a dog have Buddha-nature?' Joshu answered, 'Mu!'" "Mu" is Japanese for "no" or "no thing." Since Buddhists believe all sentient creatures possess Buddha-nature, this is an odd thing for Joshu to say. What did he mean by it? "Mu!" was Joshu's authentic expression of his understanding of Zen. What's yours? Zen students can spend weeks, months, and years keeping the sound of "mu" in awareness, in and out of meditation, until their own understanding, like a bright flash of lightning, becomes clear.

KINHIN

Kinhin is walking meditation. Zen practitioners engage in kinhin between periods of zazen. While in breath-focused zazen you focus on and return to the breath over and over, in kinhin you focus on and return to the sensations of walking. This aligns with the Zen principle of doing one thing at a time with full attention. Kinhin reminds us that we can meditate while moving, as well as while sitting still. Whatever our activity, we can always focus on our actions in the moment.

CHANTING

Zen practitioners also chant. Chants include a variety of Buddhist **sutras** (Buddhist texts), **gathas** (Buddhist poems), **mantras** (sacred phrases), and **dharanis** (incantations). These chants all have specific meanings, but the focus of chanting is on the act itself—on voicing the syllables in unison with the group. It's another opportunity to put your full attention on what you're doing in the moment. One famous Zen mantra (from the Heart Sutra) goes, "*gate, gate, paragate, parasamgate, bodhi svaha,*" which roughly translates as "gone, gone, gone beyond, gone utterly beyond, Enlightenment, svaha!" "Svaha!" is an exclamation that means something like "well said!" or "hurrah!"

SATORI

Satori is a sudden breakthrough experience that offers a taste of Enlightenment. *Kensho*, or "seeing one's true nature," is a close synonym. Satori may involve an experience of oneness with all things, a transcendence of dualistic thinking, and an awareness of all-pervading love. Satori shakes up our mistaken ideas about being small, separate selves, and opens us to our deep interconnection with the universe, an experience that transcends words. Satori is not the same as Enlightenment; it's best to think of it as a way station on the road to Enlightenment.

A State of Zen

Once we gain experience with meditation, we can begin to integrate what we've learned from it into our daily lives and, simply put, become "more Zen." These changes are reflected in how we relate to our breath, our bodies, and our minds.

BREATHING

After sufficient practice with breath-focused meditation, attention to breathing has the power to bring us into the present moment, away from preoccupations that threaten to disturb our inner peace. When we feel irritated, angry, frustrated, fearful, or sad, we can remember to take a breath and detach ourselves from the thoughts generating these negative emotions. Taking a breath gives us a "breathing space" between a difficult situation and a knee-jerk emotional reaction. It also buys us time to devise a wiser response. We become responsible rather than reactive.

BODY

Rather than living in our bodies, we can find ourselves at war with or cut off from them all too often. People might hate certain features of their bodies or live entirely in their heads. They can block out awareness of bodily sensations due to experiences of past trauma. Meditation puts us in touch with our bodies as they are in the moment. We can learn to appreciate the vibrant sensations of being alive and befriend our bodies, accepting all sensations as they come and go. As we become adept at listening to our bodies, we discover ways of knowing that precede and parallel our logical ways of knowing the world. We recover the vital heart–mind connection, so that we live in a way that fully embraces the totality of our physical and emotional being.

MIND

Our minds can be our biggest enemies. Rather than living in the present, we can dwell in regrets about the past or fears of the future. We can endlessly retell ourselves stories about people who wronged us, how great or awful we are, and what we think we need to get or get rid of in order to be happy.

Meditation teaches us that our stories are just stories and not reality. As we observe ourselves repeating the same stories over and over, we can begin to take them less seriously. We no longer

Mindfulness and Zen

Mindfulness, the act of paying attention to the present moment without judgment, is a secularized version of key Zen ideas. Mindfulness refers to:

1. Formal meditations that help us become more mindful

2. Informal awareness practices that support mindfulness throughout the day

3. Our general level of mindfulness

Research shows that therapeutic interventions such as Mindfulness-Based Stress Reduction (MBSR) and Mindfulness-Based Cognitive Therapy (MBCT) can significantly help reduce stress, pain, anxiety, and depression. Mindfulness also causes changes in areas of the brain responsible for attention and emotional regulation. Psychologists, neuropsychologists, and physicians have shown an increasing interest in mindfulness over the past two decades, and dozens of new research studies are published every month.

have to believe everything we think. As we observe our desires coming and going, we learn that we don't have to obey our every whim as if it were a command. We can better discern which urges, if pursued, lead to happiness, and which lead to trouble and misery.

The Heart of Zen

Zen is not just about cultivating awareness. It's also about developing qualities of the heart: empathy, kindness, and compassion for others with the intention of reducing whatever suffering they may be undergoing. Zen also reinforces ethical qualities such as honesty, integrity, and abstaining from harmful actions. All of this is a part of the fundamental recognition that we are all deeply interconnected.

THE ETHICAL PRECEPTS

Zen practitioners agree to abide by sixteen ethical precepts called the **bodhisattva precepts**. *Bodhisattva* means "enlightened being," and refers to practitioners who are motivated by *bodhicitta*, or the intention to liberate all beings from suffering. The precepts include vows to abstain from killing, stealing, harmful speech, sexual immorality, and indulging in intoxicants that impair judgment. Meditation alone can't lead to inner calm when one's behavior continues to stir up discord and turmoil. To attain inner harmony, we must learn how to create and sustain harmony with others. Zen students go through an intensive period of studying the bodhisattva precepts with a teacher. Students also sew a bib-like ritual garment called a *rakasu* in preparation for *jukai*, a ritual ceremony in which the teacher publicly recognizes the student's commitment to practicing the precepts.

THE BODHISATTVA VOWS

Zen practitioners vow to 1) liberate all beings from suffering, 2) end greed, hatred, and ignorance, 3) study the Buddha's teachings, and 4) strive toward Enlightenment. These vows are called the *bodhisattva vows*. A bodhisattva, in this context, isn't a fully enlightened being, but a person who has committed themself to progress on the path to Enlightenment.

THE DIVINE ABODES

Zen identifies four states of mind as the *divine abodes*: compassion, loving-kindness, equanimity, and taking joy in the good fortune of others. We try to extend kindness and compassion to everyone and rejoice in their well-being, regardless of who they are. We also strive to develop equanimity, the mental quality of composure, stability, and even-temperedness. When we have equanimity, our self-worth doesn't rise or fall based on external events. We take success and failure, praise and criticism, loss and gain in stride. Equanimity also means treating everyone the same, with kind and compassionate intentions. It doesn't mean excusing people's bad behavior, but responding effectively to it without cruel, hateful, or harmful intent.

Applying Your Practice

Once there is a basic understanding of Zen practices, how does one get started? You can begin by forming the intention to meditate regularly and by becoming more aware of the present moments that make up your life. The following tips will help you put those intentions into sustained regular practice.

DO ONE THING AT A TIME

Zen is about paying attention whole-heartedly and single-mindedly to whatever you're doing in each moment. Every activity deserves your undivided attention. Don't get lost in thinking about work or that disagreement you just had with your spouse when washing the dishes. Focus instead on the water temperature and the way your hands feel as you rinse the plates. When playing with your children, avoid distractions like thinking about making dinner or paying bills. When your mind wanders, bring it back. There is no greater gift you can give to your children than your full attention.

DEVOTE TIME TO SITTING

Carve out some time each day to meditate. If you can sit for 20 minutes or longer, great. If your schedule won't allow that much time, even 5 minutes a day can be beneficial. It can be illuminating to add up the time we spend playing games on our phones, surfing the Internet, or watching television, and experiment with devoting some of that time to sitting instead.

Try sitting at the same time each day. Set a special place aside for your meditation cushion and perhaps an altar with fresh flowers, a candle, and incense. Set the timer on your phone so you don't have to keep checking the clock. Remember to place your phone on airplane mode so you are not interrupted by phone calls and text messages.

DEVELOP RITUALS

Daily rituals can help strengthen your Zen practice. Some people begin each day by formulating a set of objectives, like the intent to meditate, be kinder, or focus more on the present moment.

Others maintain a daily loving-kindness practice of imagining family, friends, acquaintances—even people they dislike—and wishing them safety, health, and happiness. Counting your blessings daily can help you stay positive. Chanting Buddhist gathas or mantras can help increase inner calm and focus. Many people enjoy engaging in daily meditative movement practices such as yoga, tai chi, or qigong.

LIVE SIMPLY

The more we complicate our lives, the harder it is to slow down and pay attention. We can end up missing the interactions and experiences that make life worthwhile, like the warmth of a hug or the beauty of a sunset. When we allow ourselves to be driven by our desires to buy more, do more, and be more—to have more money, a bigger house, a flashier car, a thinner body, more social media attention—we find ourselves on a treadmill to nowhere.

Zen helps us step off the treadmill. It teaches us to be content with our lives as they are, and wiser about when pursuing a desire is truly in our best interest, and when it's best to just let it go.

HELP OTHERS

Zen teaches us that we're too wrapped up in ourselves. While no one can ever fulfill the bodhisattva vow to "free all beings from suffering," the vow is a reminder that not everything is about us. We begin to approach situations with an attitude of "How can I help?" rather than "What's in it for me?" Focusing more on helping others can pull us out of a self-obsessed funk and help us feel better about ourselves. The longer we travel the Zen path, the more appealing a life of service becomes.

The Benefits of Zen

While Zen recommends practicing without goals, no one would ever begin Zen practice without the hope that it might improve his or her life. Thankfully, the benefits of Zen practice are manifold. They include becoming more fully present, developing increased inner calm and stability, learning how to better accept things that can't be changed, and becoming more discerning in one's choices and actions. At more advanced stages of practice, we also develop a deeper spiritual understanding of our place in the universe.

ENLIGHTENMENT

Enlightenment means we are always aware of our deep intercon-nection with everything; freed from greed, hatred, and ignorance, and motivated by compassion to help all beings. Is Enlightenment a far-off goal we can attain only after lifetimes of practice, or is it a capacity we already possess and simply need to actualize? Is it a horizon we aim toward but never fully realize, or is it present, if only for a moment, when we sit zazen? Zen teachers have varying opin-ions on this matter.

My advice is that it's best not to practice Zen with thoughts about becoming Enlightened. Our ideas about Enlightenment only get in the way of practice; it's better to practice with the simple intent of being fully present in the moment, and see how your life changes.

PEACE

We develop inner peace when we cease struggling against life and accept it as it is. We become peaceful when we stop stirring ourselves up with thoughts of the past and future and dwell in the present. Peace comes when we remember to breathe mindfully, when our mind is focused on what we're doing right now, and when we adopt a compassionate stance and orient ourselves to helping others. All aspects of Zen work together to help us develop this inner peace.

POSITIVITY

Zen teaches a positive, life-affirming attitude. Negativity is the product of three dark thoughts: "Everything is terrible," "Nothing I do matters," and "The future looks no brighter." When we realize that these are just thoughts and not reality, we become better off. The Zen saying "Fall down seven times, get up eight," means that even if we've failed at something many times, it doesn't mean that we won't succeed next time. The key is making one's best effort, moment by moment. Just do your best.

The Japanese have a story about Uncle Sai's horse. When Uncle Sai's horse ran away, all the neighbors said, "Bad luck!" Uncle Sai replied, "Who knows?" The next day his horse returned with a mate. All the neighbors said, "Good luck!" and Uncle Sai replied, "Who knows?" The next day Uncle Sai's son fell off the new horse and broke his leg. All the neighbors said, "Bad luck!" and Uncle Sai replied, "Who knows?" The following day, soldiers came to town conscripting young men for the army. They didn't take Uncle Sai's son because his leg was broken. The Japanese say, "Everything is like Uncle Sai's horse." Even things that seem very bad can have unexpected positive outcomes. Good or bad, who knows? Just keep getting up.

COMPASSION

Compassion is the quivering of the human heart in response to suffering. Compassion isn't just a feeling, but a skill we can improve with practice. Like Dr. Seuss's Grinch, we all have hearts that are "two sizes too small" and could benefit from growing. Compassion, however, must always be coupled with wisdom. Wisdom and compassion are like the wings of a bird: a bird cannot fly without both.

Our minds tell us that certain people are undeserving of our compassion. Maybe they belong to a different ethnic group or religious faith, or we believe they stupidly caused their own suffering. Maybe they are unpleasant to be with or were cruel to us in the past. Zen says: "None of this matters." Everyone deserves our compassion, and we can't be truly happy while others around us live in suffering. We're all in this together.

BALANCE

We all want balance in our lives: between work and family, meeting our own needs and attending to the needs of others, and our private and public selves. Finding balance requires mindfulness of the subtle inner disquiet that arises when things are out of alignment. It means not shoving aside or burying our feelings, and knowing we have the right to take care of ourselves. It means attending to the social cues of other's expectations. Finally, it means compassion for ourselves and others and the equanimity to tolerate conflicting demands without reacting heedlessly. By promoting mindfulness, compassion, and equanimity, Zen gives us the tools we need to achieve greater balance.

PART TWO

EVERYDAY ZEN

Everyone can apply Zen principles to their lives regardless of personal religious beliefs. Part 2 offers Zen strategies for solving everyday problems at home, at work, or on the go. The Zen approach can be summarized in ten simple maxims: 1) Breathe/Be Mindful, 2) Be Present and Connect, 3) Accept Reality As It Is, 4) Be Kind to Yourself and Others, 5) Don't Believe All Your Thoughts, 6) Don't Be Overly Self-Centered, 7) Do What's Needed, 8) Do Your Best, Then Let Go, 9) Respect and Honor All Beings and 10) Be Upright/Maintain Integrity. The meaning of these precepts will become clear as we use them in the following chapters.

Chapter Three

ZEN AT HOME

Home is, at its best, a place of love, understanding, and support, as well as a haven from the stresses of the world. At its worst, it is a hotbed of conflict and discontent. The people we love don't always behave the way we want them to, nor do they always appreciate us the way we want to be appreciated. They may try to control us in ways we don't want to be controlled, disappoint us, or make us feel angry or inadequate. They may disappear from our lives entirely and leave us devastated.

Zen can help us through all these difficulties. It can strengthen our capacity to accept ourselves and others and help us tolerate our negative emotions while developing an inner space of calm and equanimity. It can teach us how to choose our responses wisely rather than merely reacting to situations, help us face our difficulties fearlessly, and teach us how to be more fully present with our loved ones. It can also help us realize when things are not working out and it's time to let go. The following scenarios will teach you to how to employ Zen strategies to build a more peaceful, positive, and balanced home life.

WASHING THE DISHES

Zen Maxims: Breathe/Be Mindful; Be Present/Connect; Be Kind; Don't Believe All Your Thoughts; Don't Be Self-Centered; Respect/Honor All Beings

The Problem: Couples often argue over household responsibilities. When Sam comes home from work, he expects Peg to make dinner and clean up afterward, as his mother always did. Peg also works outside the home. She doesn't mind cooking but wishes Sam would help with the dishes. Sam just wants to put his feet up after a hard day and resents being asked to do "women's work."

The Zen Approach: To resolve this the Zen way, Sam would have to take a few mindful breaths, relax, and step back to observe his thoughts. A number of his thoughts are contributing to his and Peg's inability to resolve their dispute: 1) "The way my parents did things is the way they should to be done," 2) "Washing dishes is women's work," and 3) "My desires are more important than Peg's." If he observed these thoughts, he might realize that they are not divinely given truths, but simply habits of mind. They don't have to be believed, and they don't have to interfere with finding a solution.

Sam should accept the reality that his wife works just as hard as he does. If he deserves a rest, so does she. He should remind himself that not everything in the world revolves around his own desires and that he ought to be kinder to Peg. If he can be mindful, recognize his thoughts are "just thoughts," and strive to be less self-centered and kinder, he'll be able to talk reasonably with Peg and either bow to her request or negotiate another solution.

Peg should also breathe mindfully before confronting Sam. It would be better if she accepted Sam for who he is. His upbringing has largely contributed to his way of life, and much like everyone else, he can be thoughtless and selfish at times. If she approaches him angrily, she'll just provoke defensiveness. If she can acknowledge Sam's tiredness and sympathize with his desire to rest, she'll be better able to ask him to empathize with her feelings and acknowledge her desires in return.

STUDYING FOR AN EXAM

Zen Maxims: Breathe/Be Mindful; Don't Believe All Your Thoughts; Do What's Needed; Do Your Best/Let Go

The Problem: Our emotions sometimes interfere with work that needs to be done. Greg is studying for the final exam in a class he desperately wants to pass. Whenever he tries to study, he is overwhelmed with anxiety. He reads the same paragraph in his textbook over and over without comprehension.

The Zen Approach: Greg should start with mindful breathing to calm himself. If Greg is mindful of his thoughts while breathing, he'll notice thoughts that are causing his anxiety. Rather than thinking, "I'd like to pass this exam and will work hard to do my best," he's likely thinking, "I must pass this exam or my life will be ruined," "I'm stupid if I can't pass this exam," or "My parents will be angry if I fail, and I couldn't handle that disappointment." If Greg can allow these thoughts to pass through his mind without believing them, they'll be rendered harmless. If he stops catastrophizing about how awful it would be if he failed, he'll be better able to concentrate on the task at hand, just resolving to do his best—whether it's good enough for the exam or not—and accepting the results of his effort. Once we've done our best, it's time for us to let go, whether we get the desired results or not. We can't do better than our best.

GRIEVING A LOSS

Zen Maxims: Breathe/Be Mindful; Be Present/Connect; Accept Reality; Don't Believe All Your Thoughts; Do Your Best/Let Go

The Problem: All relationships end eventually, through growing apart, conflict, or death. However, we still hope that end will be far off, or never come at all. Alexander lost his beloved wife of 35 years because of an unexpected illness. In the weeks and months after her death, he finds himself crying whenever something reminds him of his loss. He struggles to sleep at night or pay attention at work during the day. He can't imagine going on alone and can't imagine being interested in anyone else.

The Zen Approach: Alexander needs to accept that his wife is gone and has to go through the full range of feelings that loss brings. The only way out is through. He also must come to understand that if we live long enough, loss happens to us all. It's a natural part of life, and not a punishment the universe has devised just for him. He may experience thoughts like "I'll never get over this," "Happiness is over for me," "It's so unfair," or "There will never be anyone else." If he can see that these are simply thoughts, he can let them come and go without making him feel worse. Who knows what the future holds? We only know the current moment is one of grief. We can cry as long as the body feels like crying, and then be open to the next moment, which may be another moment of grief, or one of happiness or surprise: a grandchild's smile or the scent of the sea.

A HARMLESS FLIRTATION

Zen Maxims: Breathe/Be Mindful; Be Present/Connect; Don't Believe All Your Thoughts

The Problem: One person's idea of "being friendly" can be another person's idea of betrayal. Mike and Helen are at a New Year's Eve party. Mike feels neglected by Helen most of the evening as she catches up with old friends she knew before their marriage. Mike feels particularly jealous as Helen smiles and gently touches the arm of a good-looking male friend as they chat.

The Zen Approach: Mike should breathe mindfully before reacting. This will allow him to center himself, take a step back, and contemplate the situation and his reactions. He may then notice the discrepancy between the facts of the situation and his knee-jerk response.

The facts are that: 1) his wife is spending time with friends she hasn't seen in a long while, 2) she is acting friendly toward them, and 3) some of them are good-looking.

Mike's knee-jerk reactions are "She likes them better than me" and "I could lose her." These thoughts probably reflect an old habitual pattern of Mike's negative thinking about himself, maybe that he's not good-looking enough, or his personality isn't big enough to hold a woman's interest. If he can stand back and see this as an old pattern, he can observe it without acting on it. He is then free to respond to the situation in a new way, rather than reacting to it from the same old emotional space. He can pull Helen aside at some point and say, "I know it's not your fault, but I'm feeling a bit insecure. I need a hug." If he feels the need, they can also talk about it when they get home.

DECORATING

Zen Maxims: Breathe/Be Mindful; Don't Be Self-Centered; Respect/ Honor All Beings

The Problem: Working together requires mutual respect and the ability to compromise. Mia and Tom are decorating their new home. Mia has modern tastes and prefers bright, cheerful colors, while Tom prefers earth tones. They can't agree on a color scheme.

The Zen Approach: In Zen, we respect and honor everyone with a bow. Mia and Tom need to take time to mindfully get in touch with their feelings about their conflict. They should reflect on how important the color scheme is to their happiness, and how much they're willing to sacrifice for the other's happiness. Tom might ultimately care a lot less than Mia and graciously let her have her way, or Tom might care a great deal and insist on having some input. Are there potential compromises? Can they find colors that aren't quite as bright or as muted, or can some rooms be painted brightly and others in earth tones? Perhaps Mia can have her way on the color scheme, and Tom can pick accessories or even their next car? For a relationship to succeed, no person can have his or her own way all the time. Partners must learn to willingly bow to each other.

"WHY DOESN'T SHE EVER LISTEN?"

Zen Maxims: Breathe/Be Mindful; Be Present/Connect; Be Kind; Don't Believe All Your Thoughts; Don't Be Self-Centered; Respect/ Honor All Beings

The Problem: We all want to be seen, heard, and responded to in a caring way, but it doesn't always happen. Whenever Kate tells Maggie about her day, Maggie looks at her phone and says "uh-huh" without making eye contact. Kate feels ignored, unimportant, and invisible.

The Zen Approach: Kate and Maggie could both benefit from a Zen approach to improving their way of relating to each other without falling into old behavior patterns. Kate normally responds to what she considers being ignored by going into "attack mode." Attack mode usually includes "always" and "never" statements: "You always ignore me!" or "You never appreciate me." It is better to be present-centered and specific: "I'm trying to tell you about my day, but you only seem to be half listening. That makes me feel unimportant. I'd feel better if you'd put the phone down for a little while."

For Maggie's part, she needs to be more mindful of how her actions affect Kate. Specifically, she needs to be more aware of how often she is on the phone while Kate is trying to talk to her. She should ask herself, "Is what I'm currently doing on the phone more important than my partner's feelings?" Every moment offers us choices that can affect the quality of our relationships for better or worse.

When Kate tries to talk about her day, Maggie may be turning herself off with thoughts like "I've heard this all before" or "This is of little interest to me." She isn't listening freshly with beginner's mind. She also isn't listening to Kate's real message, which is "I need to feel close to you right now." She isn't responding freshly to Kate's emotional needs. No moment is an old story repeated; every moment is a new moment in which we can discover new meanings in old stories and creative ways to respond to them.

THE FAMILY BED

Zen Maxims: Breathe/Be Mindful; Be Present/Connect; Don't Believe All Your Thoughts; Don't Be Self-Centered; Respect/Honor All Beings

The Problem: Differences in parenting styles are among the most contentious marital issues. Lauren and Jason's three-year-old daughter Lila climbs into their bed when she wakes in the middle of the night. She wants to stay in their bed because she is afraid of sleeping alone in her own room. Jason is comfortable with Lila's request, but Lauren wants to put her back in her room. "You're spoiling her," she says. She feels that sharing their bed with Lila deprives them of opportunities for spontaneous intimacy.

The Zen Approach: Lauren and Jason have different opinions on handling Lila based on differences in their upbringing, differing parenting philosophies, and differing levels of concern about meeting their marital needs. Problems arise when parents think there is only one way to do things. Whatever they decide on, chances are that Lila will not be spoiled for life.

Allowing Lila into their bed has its pros and cons. On the pro side, Lauren and Jason won't have to endure her prolonged crying, and Lila won't have to suffer from being frightened in her room. On the con side, having Lila stay with them delays her ability to tolerate aloneness and interferes with Lauren and Jason's intimacy. If Lauren and Jason can talk this through calmly without accusing each other of being bad parents or not caring about each other's needs, they can arrive at a sensible compromise. Partners must learn to willingly bow to each other.

Perhaps they can let Lila into their bed for now until she's a little older or let her stay in their bed until she falls asleep, and then transfer her to her own bed. Maybe they can return her to her own bed immediately, but Lauren or Jason can stay with her until she falls asleep. The important thing is to arrive at an agreement about how to respond to Lila that satisfies them both. Doing this requires staying calm, remaining flexible, and treating each other with respect. The biggest impediments to solving this problem are being too attached to one's own opinions or too focused on one's own needs. Zen Master Bernie Glassman used to say, "Hey, it's just my opinion, man!" It's useful to remember that most of the things we believe are "just opinions" and hold them lightly.

ASSEMBLING FURNITURE

Zen Maxims: Breathe/Be Mindful; Accept Reality; Don't Believe All Your Thoughts; Do What's Needed, Do Your Best/Let Go

The Problem: Some situations are bound to cause frustration. Jacob is assembling the baby crib he bought online. The instructions are incomprehensible, there don't seem to be enough screws, and he can't seem to make the parts line up. He becomes increasingly frustrated.

The Zen Approach: Getting angry at a situation does nothing to solve it, and often just gets in the way of a resolution. Jacob should take a break from assembling the crib, breathe mindfully, and calm himself. Sometimes when we take a break, we can return to the problem later and take a fresh look at things, discovering solutions that never would have occurred to us during the moment of frustration. Maybe Jacob misunderstood the poorly worded instructions, but after taking a break, he can read them as intended. Maybe he needs to go to the hardware store and buy a couple of extra screws. Maybe the crib is defective and needs to be exchanged. It's possible to consider these things without ruining his mood. Just do what's needed, without indulging in upsetting thoughts like "I must be stupid if I can't figure this out right now," or "How dare they sell me a defective crib." Stuff happens, and not everything's easy. That's accepting reality as it is.

ENDING A RELATIONSHIP

Zen Maxims: Be Present/Connect; Be Kind; Do What's Needed; Do Your Best/Let Go; Respect/Honor All Beings; Be Upright/Maintain Integrity

The Problem: Rob and Ava have been together for six months, but lately Rob finds himself dissatisfied with their relationship. Ava seems self-absorbed and unable to give him the support he feels he needs. He wants to break up, but keeps putting it off, afraid of hurting her feelings.

The Zen Approach: Breaking up may be hard to do, but Zen asks us to step up and do what's truthful and necessary. Yes, breaking off the relationship will hurt Ava's feelings, but Rob pretending to love her when he no longer does will hurt her, too. She already senses the subtle changes in the way he responds to her, and she has been wondering what's wrong.

The Zen way is to do this as kindly as possible. Prolonging the agony or pretending things are fine isn't being kind. Telling her that their needs are not in sync and that the relationship isn't working for him—without blaming Ava—is the way to go. Zen urges us to engage in "right speech"—speech that is true, timely, apt to the situation, and kind. Zen also tells us the time to do anything is always now.

PAYING THE BILLS

Zen Maxims: Accept Reality; Don't Believe All Your Thoughts; Do What's Needed; Do Your Best/Let Go

The Problem: Paying bills every month is always a time of frustration in the Jensen household. There's never quite enough money to make ends meet. The rent is due, the car needs repair, and they'd been hoping to enroll their daughter in after-school gymnastics. Should they forget about the after-school program and contribute to the current balance owed on their credit card?

The Zen Approach: It's an unfortunate fact of life that our desires always exceed our ability to completely satisfy them. We always have to prioritize our desires, deciding which ones we'll fulfill, postpone, or forego. It becomes even more of a problem when our wants seem to be dire necessities. We all need a place to live and access to transportation.

There are long- and short-term answers to the Jensens' chronic budget shortfalls. In the long-term, are there better paying jobs they could aspire to if they received training? Could they take on an additional part-time job or two or find a place with cheaper rent? Would public transportation be more affordable than their car? Could they cut their cable bill, eat out less often, or not take a vacation? There is also the short-term decision about their daughter's gymnastics program. How much are they in debt, and how much longer would it take to pay off the added debt? Is fixing the car more important than after-school activities? Is their daughter a budding Olympic gymnast, and would skipping the class harm her future?

We can make these decisions more difficult by indulging in thoughts like "I shouldn't have to choose between these things," or "It's unfair that others have it easier." It may indeed be unfair, but that doesn't change the immediate reality they must deal with. The Jensens can work in the future toward reducing the unfairness of society, but right now, they must decide on the gymnastics class. Zen asks us to focus on doing what's necessary. Getting upset is optional and unproductive.

PARENT-TEEN CONFLICT

Zen Maxims: Breathe/Be Mindful; Be Present/Connect; Don't Be Self-Centered; Do What's Needed; Respect/Honor All Beings

The Problem: Adolescence can be hard on both parents and teenagers. Sophia is 15 years old but acts like she's 21. She doesn't think that she needs to obey the family's curfew rules and stays out as late as she wants. Her mother, feeling powerless, asks her husband to intervene. When he tells Sophia she's grounded, she defiantly tells him that he can't control her.

The Zen Approach: Sophia's father's first instinct is to respond in kind, fighting fire with fire. That will only make matters worse. He should breathe mindfully to cool down, then try his best to empathize with her feelings of being "all grown up" and wanting control over her life. He probably felt the same way at her age.

Sophia's father is still responsible for keeping his daughter safe and helping set the rules of the house. He's far from powerless. He may not be able to physically restrain Sophia, but he can withhold her allowance or confiscate her cell phone. His best option is to give Sophia and himself time to cool down before attempting a genuine conversation in which both of them can calmly and respectfully express their feelings and opinions. He must still make it clear to Sophia that her parents have the final say on the rules as long as she continues to live with them. Perhaps they will compromise on curfew hours, letting Sophia stay out longer on weekends, or devise a behavioral contract, setting clear consequences for every time Sophia breaks the rules. The Zen way is "the middle way" that balances wisdom with compassion, and strength with flexibility.

CHRONIC ILLNESS

Zen Maxims: Breathe/Be Mindful; Be Present/Connect; Accept Reality; Don't Believe All Your Thoughts; Do What's Needed

The Problem: We sometimes think our health is here to stay, but sickness can befall us at any time. James is newly diagnosed with adult-onset diabetes. He will need to control his diet, exercise more, and take medication for the rest of his life. James has always considered himself a healthy person who enjoys life to the fullest. He now must face the fact that he has a disease and must change his lifestyle.

The Zen Approach: James can approach his diagnosis as a challenge rather than a catastrophe. If he learns how to control his blood sugar by following a diabetic diet, exercising, and taking his medication properly, he can avoid many, if not most, of the complications of the disease. His thoughts are the only thing preventing James from successfully meeting this challenge. These include denying that he is really sick, resenting the loss of his perceived perfect health, and thinking he can still eat any way he likes. Zen calls for acceptance of the situation. Anger, resentment, grief, defiance, and denial will only make James sicker. He needs to do what's needed to care for himself. This means doing what Zen calls "urge surfing": when the urge to eat something he shouldn't arises, he can close his eyes and meditate on the urge, watching it come and go without acting on it. Urges don't control us unless we let them. When we understand them as transient phenomena, we can observe them without needing to act on them.

THE AGING PARENT

Zen Maxims: Breathe/Be Mindful; Accept Reality; Be Kind; Don't
Believe All Your Thoughts; Don't Be Self-Centered; Do What's
Needed; Do Your Best/Let Go; Be Upright/Maintain Integrity

The Problem: Life has a way of handing us responsibilities whether
we want them or not. Kevin's father, Jack, is showing signs of
dementia and can't live independently anymore. Kevin and his wife
have a high-school-aged daughter still at home, and Jack isn't the
easiest person to get along with. Jack says he'd "rather die" than
go into assisted living, and there isn't money available to pay for it
anyway. Should they invite Jack to live with them?

The Zen Approach: The family can pay for 24-hour home care at
Jack's place, invite him to live with them, or leave him in a situation
where he's at constant risk of injury or death. If the money isn't
there for home care, and if Kevin and his wife have a conscience,
they have no choice but to invite him into their home. This will mean
considerable inconvenience and disruption in their daily routines.
Someone will always have to be home with him. Jack's cantankerous
manner is bound to fray nerves and put everyone on edge.

Several Zen skills can help Kevin and his family cope with this
situation. The first is acceptance, that this is the way it is, whether
they like it or not. This includes accepting Jack's personality as it
is. He is set in his ways and has lost much of his mental capacity.
There's no value to be gained in thinking "How dare he? He should

be different!" These thoughts only fuel anger and resentment while doing nothing to change Jack. Whenever Jack says something particularly egregious and Kevin asks, "Must I accept this, too?" the answer is "Yes, this, too." Kevin should meditate to find the peace of mind that is attainable in nearly every situation. As in every situation, the Zen attitude is "Do your best, and then let go."

FEAR OF DATING

Zen Maxims: Breathe/Be Mindful; Be Present/Connect; Accept Reality; Don't Believe All Your Thoughts; Do Your Best/Let Go

The Problem: Kyle and his wife recently divorced. He wants companionship but is afraid to get back into the dating scene. He's still feeling bruised from the failure of his marriage, and the rules of dating have changed quite a bit since he was younger. He's always been shy, self-conscious about his looks, and doesn't have much money left over after alimony. He worries he doesn't have a lot to offer a woman.

The Zen Approach: Kyle can meditate to observe his fearful thoughts without believing in them. His hesitation and fear are consequences of thoughts like "Given my shyness, mediocre looks, and finances, no woman will ever love me" or "I'll never be able to learn the new dating rules." These are all mental projections onto a future that hasn't happened yet. It's possible that a woman will love Kyle for his kindness, sense of responsibility, and good humor. Just because things didn't work out with his wife doesn't mean they won't work out with someone else. Once he stops mistaking his thoughts for reality, he's free to step into the future with a beginner's mind, encountering successes and failures as he learns the new dating rules, doing his best moment by moment, and letting go of the need for certainty and control over outcomes.

UNWANTED ADVANCES

Zen Maxims: Breathe/Be Mindful; Be Present/Connect; Be Kind; Don't Be Self-Centered; Do What's Needed; Be Upright/Maintain Integrity

The Problem: Sarah is shocked when her best friend Amy's husband suggests they leave a crowded dinner party to get some "quiet time together." Sarah wonders how to send a clear message to Ted that she will not tolerate his unwelcome advances and whether she should tell Amy.

The Zen Approach: Sarah needs to send an unequivocal message to Ted that his inappropriate behavior was unacceptable through her choice of words, tone of voice, facial expression, and body language. This means being fully present in the moment and not undercutting her message by vacillating or minimizing. Her communication should leave no doubt about where she stands.

Whether to tell Amy is a more complex question. If Amy doesn't believe Sarah, it could damage their friendship. But is it fair to Amy to keep her husband's suggestive language from her? It's also possible that Amy suspects her husband's unfaithfulness, and Sarah's information could help empower Amy to confront him.

Zen says we shouldn't say potentially hurtful things just because they happen to be true. We should only do so when the timing is right and our words are likely to be helpful. Sarah should mindfully contemplate how she might feel if she were Amy. Would she want to know if she were in Amy's shoes? She should also consider if revealing this information will end their friendship. She shouldn't proceed until she's willing to risk losing her best friend and feels that the information is likely to help Amy.

INTERNET BULLYING

Zen Maxims: Breathe/Be Mindful; Be Present/Connect; Accept Reality; Don't Believe All Your Thoughts; Do What's Needed; Do Your Best/Let Go

The Problem: Noah is a 14-year-old gender-nonconforming person whose preferred pronouns are "she" and "her." Classmates have been calling her names on social media and suggesting that others shun her.

The Zen Approach: Social ostracism can cause profound psychological harm, and a 14-year-old is especially vulnerable to it. It may be hard for Noah to understand at this age that "this too shall pass," and to disregard her classmates' taunts that something is profoundly "wrong" with her. Hopefully she has parents, mentors, or allies who can prevent her from feeling isolated and alone.

Noah should close her social media accounts to prevent her from being subjected to continued online harassment and seek support through a peer-support group or LGBTQ-friendly supportive counseling in the community. Noah can also meet with adult or peer allies (if they exist) and inform school authorities about the harassment and ostracism from her classmates. The authorities should confront her harassers, enforce consequences for their behavior, offer supportive counseling for Noah, and take steps to educate the school community about gender identity. These interventions, of course, depend on Noah's school district's willingness to support her.

Noah can also use Zen meditation to help accept a life situation she can do little to change. Meditation can help her hold her hurt and anger in a larger container of equanimity, allowing her to experience her feelings without being overwhelmed by them. When thoughts come to mind like "There's something wrong with me," "I'll never have friends," or "This will go on forever," she can observe them, and let them go. If she can accept her situation without embracing negative self-concepts, she'll be free to move forward positively, working with others to build a future in which everyone is shown respect and dignity.

IN-LAW PROBLEM

Zen Maxims: Breathe/Be Mindful; Be Present/Connect; Accept Reality; Do Your Best/Let Go

The Problem: Ethan and Linda got along fine until Linda's mother came to stay with them for the holidays. Linda's mom is, in her own words, "just trying to be helpful," making numerous suggestions for improving their housekeeping and childcare. Ethan resents her intrusion, and Linda feels she is constantly being judged by her mother.

The Zen Approach: Zen endorses the Serenity Prayer idea that we should change what we can, accept what we can't change, and understand the difference between the two. Ethan and Linda should sit down with Linda's mother and respectfully let her know how her comments make them feel. They might choose to say, "I know you're only trying to be helpful, but when you say 'X,' it makes me feel 'Y.'" This statement avoids personally attacking Linda's mother and acknowledges the possibility that her suggestions are well-intended while clearly informing her how her comments negatively affect them.

After having done their best, Ethan and Linda need to let go and accept that their intervention may not be completely successful. They must recognize that Linda's mother is only there for the holidays and that they should accept that she, like everyone else, is imperfect. Whenever she makes a cringeworthy comment, they can mindfully breathe and let it pass. Also, who knows? Some of Linda's mother's suggestions may actually be useful, if Linda is able to listen to them with fresh ears.

LONELY AND ISOLATED

Zen Maxims: Breathe/Be Mindful; Be Present/Connect; Accept Reality; Don't Believe All Your Thoughts; Do What's Needed

The Problem: Debra lives alone and works at a time-consuming, stressful job far from where she was born and raised. She moved to this new city about a year ago and still hasn't made new friends. The phone never rings, and she feels lonely and isolated.

The Zen Approach: Debra's first task is to learn how to accept and tolerate the feelings of loneliness without telling herself that it's her fault she's alone, or that it will always be this way—it's just the way things are right now. Meditation can help Debra experience her feelings without being overwhelmed by them. It takes time to find friends in a new city, especially when one's job is all-consuming.

After accepting her feelings, Debra needs to think through her options. Should she look for a less time-consuming job? Move back to her hometown where she had friends? Sign up for a class, join a club, or start a reading group at the local library? Her imagination is her only limit, once she finds the courage to take the first step.

OVEREATING

Zen Maxims: Breathe/Be Mindful; Be Present/Connect; Don't Believe All Your Thoughts; Do What's Needed

The Problem: Oliver is stressed by his job. He lives alone, spending most of his down time in front of the television or playing video games. He finds himself mindlessly devouring cartons of ice cream and bags of chips just to experience some pleasure in his life but ends up feeling worse afterward. "Why can't I show some willpower?" he moans.

The Zen Approach: Instead of solving the problems that are genuinely contributing to his stress, Oliver is attempting to use short-term forms of relief that are ultimately making him feel worse. The first thing he should do is meditate to lessen his experience of stress. He can do this by simply following his breath (see breath-focused meditation in chapter 2) for 20 minutes a day rather than playing video games. He will probably begin feeling calmer within a week or two. As he meditates, he may discover thoughts that contribute to his work-related stress. His social isolation outside of work may be another source of stress. If so, he can seek out social activities that will be more intrinsically rewarding than his current passive solitary pursuits and help him develop new friendships.

Oliver is trying to fill his emotional emptiness with empty calories. He blames his binge eating on a lack of willpower, but when he's calmer and engaged in more rewarding activities with others, his need for junk food may diminish, and he'll be better able to set goals for himself. If those foods aren't in the house, he won't be as tempted by them, so the most important time for him to exercise discipline is while grocery shopping. He can make a shopping list, being mindful to put only healthy things on it, and then buy only what's on the list, rather than making impulse purchases. Oliver's real problem is that his life is adrift. Zen asks us to step up and be fully present in our lives, moment after moment.

QUITTING SMOKING

Zen Maxims: Breathe/Be Mindful; Be Present/Connect; Do What's Needed

The Problem: Some things that feel good are not good for us. Jennifer started smoking in college while trying to lose weight and study for exams. Five years later, she smokes two packs a day. She and her husband are trying to have a child, and Jennifer knows that she doesn't want to smoke if she gets pregnant as it's unhealthy for the baby. She's tried several times to quit, but after a few days, her urge to smoke becomes too strong and she relapses.

The Zen Approach: Jennifer should begin by acknowledging that quitting is hard, and there is no reason to beat herself up over past failures. She just needs extra help. There are smoking cessation programs, support groups, and medications she may find helpful.

Zen also has some useful tricks up its sleeve. The first is to learn that urges to smoke are transient, and no matter how strong they are, Jennifer won't die if she resists them—she'll just be temporarily uncomfortable. She can master this acknowledgment by being mindful of her urges as they arise and observing them until they pass of their own accord. Each time she successfully resists an urge, it's like strengthening a muscle. It will also be easier to resist her urges if she gets rid of all the cigarettes in her house and doesn't keep some around "in case of emergency."

One reason quitting smoking is so hard is because its pleasures are immediate, while its dangers lie far in the future. This can be counteracted though visualization; before finally quitting, Jennifer can meditate while smoking, imagining how each puff is soiling her lungs and activating cancer cells. She can also visualize what it might do to her future child during pregnancy. If she can visualize this again and again, puff after puff, the pleasure of smoking will decrease, and quitting will be easier.

NOISY NEIGHBOR

Zen Maxims: Breathe/Be Mindful; Be Present/Connect; Do What's Needed; Be Kind; Respect/Honor All Beings

The Problem: The Smiths live in an apartment with their one-year-old daughter. A new renter just moved in to the upstairs apartment. He plays his stereo loudly at all hours of the day and night, so no one in the Smith family is getting much sleep.

The Zen Approach: What could be stopping the Smiths from telling their neighbor how his noise is bothering them? Perhaps they imagine scenarios in which he responds angrily to their complaint, threatens to make their life more miserable, or just ignores them? Maybe they're unassertive and risk-averse, and the thought of speaking with him fills them with dread and anxiety. This scenario is an instance of letting fear get in the way of doing what's necessary. They can't control how their neighbor will respond, but they are responsible for telling their own truth, and they need to stop procrastinating. Zen courage is doing what's necessary even when afraid—just do it! They should be respectful and kind when telling their neighbor how much his noise is disturbing them. Even people who make our lives miserable deserve the basic respect due to all sentient beings. Their neighbor can listen to his music with headphones if he doesn't want to lower the volume, and if he unreasonably refuses to accommodate their request, they can call the landlord.

THAT DARN COMPUTER!

Zen Maxims: Breathe/Be Mindful; Accept Reality; Be Kind; Don't Believe All Your Thoughts; Respect/Honor All Beings

The Problem: Aileen is trying to log on to her banking site, but it won't accept her password. After three tries, she is locked out. She calls customer service to reset her password and gives the representative an earful. Why must using the computer always be so frustrating?

The Zen Approach: Aileen is dealing with the frustration many of us feel when tasks that we imagined being simple and straightforward end up being complex and time-consuming. "This should be easy!" or "I don't have the time to waste on this!" or "I can't believe I have to go through this again!" are thoughts that intensify this frustration. It would be ideal if life were easier and we never had to waste our time, but it isn't easy, and certain tasks take time. Technology may allow us to do away with passwords someday, but for now we're stuck with them. Acceptance is a better strategy than anger. The customer service representative didn't invent the system and doesn't deserve her bad temper. Instead of blowing up, Aileen should take a few mindful breaths and bow to reality.

OBSESSIVE WORRYING

Zen Maxims: Breathe/Be Mindful; Accept Reality; Don't Believe
All Your Thoughts

The Problem: Alex can't relax. He worries about every detail of
his life, vividly imagining everything that could go wrong with any
course of action he takes. He finds himself paralyzed and unable to
get started with almost everything.

The Zen Approach: The kind of generalized anxiety disorder that
Alex seems to exhibit can first be helped by psychotherapy and/or
medication, but the Zen approach of recognizing that we don't have
to believe or act on our thoughts can also help. If Alex meditated, he
could observe these rampant worrying thoughts in his consciousness. If he could view them as clouds scuttling across the blue sky
of consciousness, watching them come and go without getting
caught up in them, they might lose some of their commanding force.
The trick is to observe them with equanimity, remaining unaffected.
Wishing them away won't help, but learning to accept them without
identifying with them can.

LETTING GO

Zen Maxims: Breathe/Be Mindful; Don't Believe All Your Thoughts; Do What's Needed

The Problem: Jamie finds it hard to throw anything away. Her dining room table is cluttered with mail and old newspapers, her kitchen cabinets with empty jars and containers, and her garage with pairs of worn-out shoes. Whenever she considers throwing anything away, she reminds herself that "I never know when it might come in useful." Her friends are secretly on the verge of staging an intervention.

The Zen Approach: Jamie's thoughts, "This might come in useful one day" and "If something might be useful, it would be a tragedy to throw it away," are central to the problem. Some of her possessions might turn out to be useful, but how often has she needed old newspapers and worn-out shoes? Even if it turns out that a newspaper might have turned out useful, how awful would it be—on an awfulness scale of 0 to 100—to have thrown it out? Each time Jamie forms the intention to pitch some clutter, she should observe her problematic thoughts with equanimity, take a mindful breath, and discard it.

OVERTHINKING CONFRONTATION

Zen Maxims: Breathe/Be Mindful; Don't Believe All Your Thoughts; Do What's Needed; Do Your Best/Let Go; Respect/Honor All Beings

The Problem: Liam wants to tell his best friend Don to stop asking him for money, but frets over the best way to say it. Don already owes him money that he has shown no sign of paying back. Liam likes Don and doesn't want to lose him as a friend. He keeps rehearsing possible approaches but can't seem to settle on one.

The Zen Approach: Liam has two goals: getting his money back and retaining Don's friendship. His belief that there is one perfect way to communicate this information, and he must find it, is stopping him. In reality, there is rarely one perfect way to do anything, and most of what we do is never "perfect"—only more or less adequate. The important thing is to do our best—sometimes failing, sometimes succeeding, sometimes just muddling through.

Liam needs to get on with it. He should approach Don respectfully and kindly, reminding him of the owed debt. Hopefully Don will pay up, but Liam can't control this outcome. If Don decides to end the friendship, so be it. Liam doesn't need friends who take advantage of him, however charming they may be, and perhaps Liam is overestimating Don's importance as a friend in the first place. Zen teaches that when we set up perfectionistic standards for how we must perform and how things must turn out, we create problems for ourselves. We must just do our best each moment as it comes.

DUMPED

Zen Maxims: Be Present/Connect; Accept Reality; Don't Believe All Your Thoughts; Do Your Best/Let Go

The Problem: Charles was shocked when Lori suddenly ended their relationship after five months and began dating someone else. He can't accept their relationship is over and keeps contacting her to beg her to change her mind and come back.

The Zen Approach: Charles's problematic thoughts are "I can't believe it's over," "I can't accept this," and "There can be no happiness after Lori." Over seven billion people in the world currently live just fine without Lori, so the odds are that Charles can, too. The main issue here is one of acceptance and letting go. So much of life fails to go the way we would like it to, and because of this, we have to bow to reality over and over again. Zen tells us that pain and suffering are an inevitable part of life. Charles has to accept and grieve his loss if he's going to heal. Living fully means accepting all the joys and suffering life brings our way. Tears and heartache are part of the package.

Chapter Four

ZEN AT WORK

We want our work to be meaningful, useful, interesting, well-compensated, and suited to our abilities—after all, we spend roughly half of our waking hours there. We also desire wise bosses, cooperative coworkers, opportunities to make a difference and for advancement, and recognition and appreciation from others. We hope that our careers aren't so demanding that they deprive us of time for love, family, recreation, relaxation, creativity, and personal development.

We often get less than we hope for in work. We might get stuck in positions where we're underappreciated and undercompensated, with limited chances for advancement. We can labor at jobs that are boring and meaningless. Our bosses can be cruel, capricious, and abusive, and our coworkers uncooperative, resentful, and spiteful. We can be overworked, overstressed, and laid off without warning. Zen can be a steady rudder to keep us on course as we navigate the ups and downs that are a part of any job. It can help us stay balanced, focused, emotionally engaged, and effective at work.

This chapter illustrates ways to incorporate Zen practices in situations at work. Once again, I have distilled the essence of Zen into ten simple maxims: 1) Breathe/Be Mindful, 2) Be Present and Connect, 3) Accept Reality As It Is, 4) Be Kind to Yourself and Others, 5) Don't Believe All Your Thoughts, 6) Don't Be Self-Centered, 7) Do What's Needed, 8) Do Your Best, Then Let Go, 9) Respect and Honor All Beings, and 10) Be Upright/Maintain Integrity.

THE TO-DO LIST

Zen Maxims: Breathe/Be Mindful; Don't Believe All Your Thoughts; Do Your Best/Let Go

The Problem: Pat has just returned to the office after vacation and is overwhelmed by her to-do list. She has hundreds of e-mails to respond to, significant issues with important clients that require resolution, and her boss wants a report on his desk by the end of the week. She can't possibly do it all.

The Zen Approach: The trick here is to take a few mindful breaths, then prioritize. Some things are more important than others: some things must be done right away, others can wait, and still others may not be worth her attention at all. There are only so many hours in the day, and Pat can only do so much. While some things may need to be done as perfectly as possible, others may require only a minimal effort.

Pat's peace of mind may be disturbed by the thought "I must get it all done or else." She should allow that thought to come and go without believing in it, focusing instead on doing her best, and not worrying so much about what others think. She can't do any better than her best, and worrying is a waste of energy. She can only control her own actions and has no control over other's reactions. If someone is upset that she didn't get back to them in a timely fashion, it can't be helped. She can always apologize to them, but there is no reason for self-reproach.

MISCOMMUNICATION

Zen Maxims: Breathe/Be Mindful; Be Present/Connect; Don't Believe All Your Thoughts

The Problem: When Paul sent out a group e-mail about an important meeting, he inadvertently left Richard off the circulation list. Richard wonders whether this action was an intentional slight.

The Zen Approach: Richard should take a few mindful breaths and recognize the thought "They left me off on purpose" is just a thought. He shouldn't spend time letting it incubate and fester into an unproven certainty. He should contact Paul right away and ask if there was a reason he was left off the e-mail chain, or whether it was an oversight. He should take care to ask in a neutral, nonaccusatory manner without overt resentment or anxiety. It's important to nip insecurity in the bud before it grows into paranoia. The best way to do that is by performing a "reality check"—checking in with the person we feel slighted by.

MANAGING E-MAILS

Zen Maxims: Breathe/Be Mindful; Do What's Needed; Do Your Best/Let Go

The Problem: If Heather responded to every e-mail she received, she'd never have time to do the rest of her job. Heather has been feeling overwhelmed ever since her department downsized a few months ago and, as a result, she was assigned additional responsibility. She stares at her overfull inbox in disbelief. She considers ignoring it all; maybe it will just go away.

The Zen Approach: Of course, the e-mails won't just go away. The first step in tackling an overwhelming task is to take a few mindful breaths to bring down her level of anxiety. Heather should estimate how much time she can realistically give to her e-mails, and then do what she can within that time frame. They may not all need a response—or at least not a lengthy one. For some recipients, a simple acknowledgment of receipt may be satisfactory. Other e-mails may contain information sent to all employees that does not require a personal response and can be read later. Heather should prioritize the most urgent e-mails and respond to them first. When the time she's allotted for responding to the e-mails runs out, she should put the rest aside until higher priority work is completed first and she has time left over. E-mails that have not yet been responded to will just have to wait. This is how overwhelming tasks get done—little by little, one step at a time. Don't get overwhelmed by looking at how high the mountain is. Look right in front of you and take the next step.

MEETING DEADLINES

Zen Maxims: Breathe/Be Mindful; Accept Reality; Don't Believe All Your Thoughts; Don't Be Self-Centered

The Problem: Chris has always been a spontaneous, creative type who works best on projects that interest and excite him. When tasks are boring and ungratifying, he waits until the last minute to work on them. He then feels the pressure of being unable to satisfactorily complete them by their deadlines.

The Zen Approach: The Zen way is "When working just work; when doing nothing, just do nothing." Procrastinating, on the other hand, is neither truly working nor genuinely enjoying idleness. Chris's problem is both a failure to accept reality as it is and an overvaluing of the importance of his desires. It's natural to prefer that things always be interesting and gratifying, but irrational to demand they always be that way. We don't always get to set the conditions under which we must work.

Chris should contemplate his thoughts about procrastination, such as "A creative person like me shouldn't have to do boring work." He should ask himself whether these thoughts are reasonable and helpful. Do they lead to happiness and fulfillment, or stress and failure? Much of Zen practice is learning to discriminate between thoughts that help us and thoughts that hurt us. Once Chris develops the insight that believing in his procrastination-generating thoughts only leads to increased stress and poorer performance, he can let go of these thoughts when they occur and focus on being effective.

COWORKER CONFLICT

Zen Maxims: Breathe/Be Mindful; Be Present/Connect; Accept Reality; Respect/Honor All Beings

The Problem: William and Brian share overlapping responsibilities on their company's organizational chart. Things won't get done unless they cooperate, but Brian is unpleasant to work with. He is quick-tempered, rude, and domineering.

The Zen Approach: Unless William can get his boss to redraw the organizational chart, he must accept working with Brian. He should take a few mindful breaths and remind himself that he doesn't have to like everyone he works with. Brian may be unpleasant, but they don't have to be friends; they only need to develop a functional working relationship.

William also needs to remind himself that everyone, no matter how awful, deserves the basic respect due all sentient beings. Finally, when Brian is being unusually offensive, William should calmly but firmly let him know he's causing friction and unnecessary ill will, and making it harder for them to work together: "I always try to show you respect, and I hope you'll try harder to do the same."

If Brian continues to behave poorly despite William's efforts to be civil and set boundaries, it may be time to report Brian to his supervisor or Human Resources. If nothing changes, William can only bow to the situation and work at improving his tolerance skills. Ill-tempered rudeness is never pleasant, but it's not as bad as being boiled in oil or catching the bubonic plague. William needs to put Brian's behavior in perspective.

THE UNAPPRECIATIVE BOSS

Zen Maxims: Breathe/Be Mindful; Be Present/Connect; Accept Reality; Don't Believe All Your Thoughts

The Problem: Irene likes her colleagues and her job, but her boss is extremely difficult to work with and she sometimes feels like quitting. He never shows appreciation for anything she does no matter how well she performs. He also never fails to criticize tiny details about her work.

The Zen Approach: Irene must consider how important various factors are to her overall well-being. If the job pays well and she likes everything about it besides her boss's poor interpersonal skills, maybe she can accept that there's no such thing as a job where everything and everyone is perfect. If she leaves this job for another, there will be imperfect things about her next opportunity, too.

How important is her boss's appreciation to her well-being? If it signals the likelihood of her getting a raise, it may be very important. If the boss treats everyone this way, it may signify nothing. If she rarely interacts with her boss, perhaps this doesn't have to be such a major issue.

On the other hand, her boss's failure to express appreciation may trigger memories of others not appreciating her. Perhaps her parents were stingy in expressing their love, and her boss's behavior triggers habitual reactive thought patterns, like "I must be inadequate," and "I can't stand that I'm never appreciated." If Irene can mindfully observe these thoughts and feelings, perhaps she can allow them to come and go without letting them trigger major emotional upset.

Finally, there's the possibility that Irene's boss is not such a bad guy, simply thoughtless about how he affects people. Irene might suggest to him in a review that he'd be a more effective manager if he sometimes balanced criticism with praise. Irene should only attempt this if she has evidence that her advice might be received in the spirit in which it was given.

BEING ORDERED TO BEHAVE UNETHICALLY

Zen Maxims: Be Present/Connect; Do What's Needed; Do Your Best/ Let Go; Be Upright/Maintain Integrity

The Problem: Eli's boss instructed him to fudge a financial report to investors. "Don't worry," the boss says. "We're just covering up a temporary shortfall that we'll more than make up for next quarter."

The Zen Approach: It's easy for the boss to say, "Don't worry," but he is asking Eli to put his integrity, accounting license, livelihood, and perhaps even freedom from prosecution on the line. Of course, if he refuses, he may be putting his future with the company on the line.

It could be easy under these circumstances to "go with the flow" and convince himself of the boss's definition of reality: "It's no big deal. Everyone does it." Except it *is* important, and many people *don't* do it. Eli knows it's not only unprofessional, but wrong.

Eli should inform his boss that he's unwilling to fudge the financial report. Then, if he isn't immediately fired, he should start looking for another job. This means a willingness to accept the consequences of his actions. Maybe finding another job will be hard, or maybe the one he finds won't pay as well. Maybe his friends will think he's been foolish. On the other hand, he gets to keep his self-esteem and escape legal repercussions.

What Eli doesn't need to do is make things worse by bemoaning the unfairness of the world: "It's unfair that I'm being asked to pay a price for being honest." Life is unfair, and we can't demand that the world be better than it is. We can only be responsible for our own behavior, and after doing our best, let go and accept reality as it is.

COWORKER JEALOUSY

Zen Maxims: Breathe/Be Mindful; Be Present/Connect; Accept Reality; Be Kind; Respect/Honor All Beings

The Problem: Ever since Megan got a promotion, Rebecca has treated her coolly. She's shut her out of her confidences and doesn't make eye contact.

The Zen Approach: When good things happen for us, not everyone rejoices for us. Others will possibly resent that our good fortune wasn't theirs instead. This is an unfortunate truth about the world that Megan would be better off accepting rather than allowing it to plague her.

If Megan can accept this, the next question is how important Rebecca's behavior is to her well-being. Rebecca may be a somewhat peripheral person to Megan, and her poor attitude only a minor inconvenience. If so, each time Rebecca ignores her, Megan should just take a few mindful breaths, accept it, and let it go.

On the other hand, Megan may have valued her past relationship with Rebecca, and it may be important to her to try to salvage it. In that case, it makes sense to try to pull her aside and have a conversation. Megan should maintain an attitude of respect and kindness throughout their conversation regardless of how Rebecca behaves. She can begin by saying, "I've always valued our friendship, but since I've been promoted, I've noticed you've cooled to me. I'm not sure why. I'd like to know if there's any way we can be friends again." If Rebecca is uninterested in restoring friendly relations, there's nothing more Megan can do other than accept it.

ASKING FOR A RAISE

Zen Maxims: Breathe/Be Mindful; Be Present/Connect; Do Your Best/Let Go

The Problem: Andy's been working for the company for over a year. His performance reviews have been excellent, but he recently discovered that newer hires are making more money than he is.

The Zen Approach: It's only natural that Andy's upset. Who wouldn't be? But before he swings into action, he should take a few mindful breaths and cool down. Then he'll be better able to devise an effective strategy that increases his chances of getting a raise.

He shouldn't be shy about talking with his boss, but before he does, he should line up the facts supporting his argument. His manner of presentation should be professional, calm, and respectful. If his boss refuses, he should ask for the reasons why. That will help Andy decide on his next step. He can make a complaint to Human Resources or the state Labor Relations Board, begin looking for another job, or just learn to accept things as they are.

It helps to stay in the moment, taking each step one at a time, and not getting caught up in imagining what might happen down the road. Imagining what might happen next and becoming upset about what may never, in fact, occur is one sure way to make Andy even more stressed out. If we take care of each present moment, the future takes care of itself.

SUPERVISING FORMER COWORKERS

Zen Maxims: Breathe/Be Mindful; Accept Reality; Do Your Best/Let Go

The Problem: Jeff used to be part of the crew on the loading dock but recently has been promoted to foreman. He wrote up Steve, a former crewmate, for taking too much time on break. Steve asks, "What happened to you? You used to be decent enough, but now you're just one of them."

The Zen Approach: It can be hard for former peers to accept your new authority. Every promotion risks disturbing old relationships. Jeff feels torn by Steve's criticism. He likes Steve, and hates having Steve be angry at him. On the other hand, if he's to succeed in his new role, Jeff must make it clear that he intends to exercise his authority properly.

Steve's comment is a manipulative challenge to Jeff's new role, and Jeff has to be up to the task of reinforcing the lines of authority. Jeff must accept whatever sadness and distress he feels at having his old pal be angry at him, while remaining steadfast. The Zen way is to be mindful of feelings, but also accepting that this is the way things are. He should tell Steve he takes his new supervisory role seriously, and that he intends to do his job fairly to the best of his ability.

FIRING AN EMPLOYEE

Zen Maxims: Breathe/Be Mindful; Accept Reality; Be Kind; Do Your Best/Let Go

The Problem: Kayla was initially pleased when she hired Anna, an acquaintance from church. However, Anna has proven to be a lackluster employee, and has shown she's not the right person for the job.

The Zen Approach: Kayla feels the conflict between her ties of acquaintanceship with Anna and her supervisory role. She should mindfully acknowledge that tension to herself. It's never pleasant telling someone they're being terminated. This is especially true when you have a relationship with that person outside of a work setting. Kayla will still see Anna at church even though there will now be tension between them. Who knows whether Anna will bad-mouth her to the other members of their congregation?

On the other hand, Kayla has a primary responsibility for the success of her company, and that mission takes priority. If she's sure Anna's not right for the job, she shouldn't delay terminating her. She should be mindful of her mixed emotions but accept the necessity of acting in the best interest of the company. She should be as kind as possible in conveying the news to Anna, expressing the hope that they can remain on good terms outside of work. Having done her best, Kayla has to then let go. She can't control Anna's reaction to being fired, or what Anna says about her at church. This means accepting any fallout that comes with equanimity.

HELP IS NOT ON THE WAY

Zen Maxims: Accept Reality; Do Your Best/Let Go

The Problem: Ed can only manage his and his team's contributions; he has no control over the outcome. His team has been working overtime, but there's no way they can get everything done by launch day. He needs more help, but the company's put a freeze on hiring.

The Zen Approach: Ed is in an uncomfortable position. His future in the company depends on the success of this project, but he's not going to get the support he needs. All Ed can do is try his best. If he and his team work hard, perhaps the product launch will go well. Perhaps it won't.

Ed can only do his best; he can't control the outcome. Sure, it's unjust, but under these circumstances, it does no good to get upset over the unfairness of the situation. He needs to put his head down, focus, and deal with it. Of course, he should also protect himself by documenting his concerns and requests for additional help.

COUNSELING AN EMPLOYEE

Zen Maxims: Breathe/Be Mindful; Be Present/Connect; Be Kind

The Problem: Molly's new hire, Gail, is floundering at her job. While she seemed sharp and well-motivated at first, she now seems withdrawn and unfocused. Molly recently overheard Gail crying in the restroom. She wonders whether Gail is struggling with personal issues that are impairing her performance.

The Zen Approach: Gail's issues are her private concern and would ordinarily be none of Molly's business. However, since these issues are now affecting Gail's job performance, they've become Molly's concern. Molly should have a private conference with Gail to share her observations. She should recommend Gail seek help, either privately or through the employee assistance program.

The important thing is for Molly to be sympathetic and supportive. She isn't meeting with Gail to criticize her performance, but to encourage her to seek help, without prying into Gail's matters. She should permit Gail to share as much or as little of what's going on as she wishes. Molly isn't there to be a counselor or confidante, and Gail should be sharing her personal issues with a therapist and not her boss. Molly doesn't want this to turn into a relationship where Gail is constantly turning to her for emotional support. After Molly shares her concerns and gives her recommendations, it's up to Gail to follow through. If she doesn't get help and doesn't improve, Molly may have to let her go.

Throughout all this, Molly needs to be mindful of her responsibilities to both the business and to Gail, as well as her professional boundaries. There are powerful psychological forces (empathy for Gail, fear of being intrusive, uncertainty about how to handle emotional problems) that may cause Molly to be less effective than she would be in other situations. Molly needs to breathe mindfully, notice these psychological forces as they arise, and stay focused on the goals appropriate to her role.

WORK/LIFE BALANCE

Zen Maxims: Breathe/Be Mindful; Be Present/Connect; Accept Reality; Don't Believe All Your Thoughts; Do Your Best/Let Go

The Problem: Kelly, a mother of two, re-entered the workforce when her husband's factory closed and his new job no longer covered the bills. Between working, maintaining a home, and raising children, she's tired all the time. There's no time left over for self-care or attending to her relationship with her husband.

The Zen Approach: Kelly is too busy to sit down and meditate, but no matter how busy she is, she can always take a minute throughout her day to breathe mindfully. She can use spontaneous reminders like a phone ringtone or a washing machine chime as cues to stop whatever she's doing and take a mindful breath. These mindful moments can put her in touch with the peace that's almost always available when we fully invest our attention in the present. We endure repetitive tasks all too often by daydreaming about something else while doing them. Investing renewed attention in whatever we're doing allows us to savor the sensations accompanying our activity.

Kelly can also benefit from adjusting her expectations. She should allow thoughts like "My house must be perfect" to come and go without believing them. She should accept that her house is inevitably going to be less neat and orderly now that she's working outside of the home. If her family wants the house to be more like it used to be, she can ask them to help more around the house now that she is working and cannot devote the time to it that she used to.

Kelly can reassure her husband that her decreased romantic interest isn't his fault. She still loves him but is exhausted by her new schedule. If they can discuss their feelings without blame or shame, they may discover new ways of interacting that can restore some of their previous connection. Kelly and her husband both need to work at accepting this is the way things are for now, and while it may not be ideal, they can find ways to live with it.

SEXUAL HARASSMENT

Zen Maxims: Be Present/Connect; Accept Reality; Do Your Best/Let Go; Be Upright/Maintain Integrity

The Problem: Jody's boss keeps making inappropriate comments about how attractive she is. Today he asked her to accompany him on a weekend business trip.

The Zen Approach: Jody isn't interested in a sexual relationship with her boss. She wants to put a firm stop to his behavior but doesn't want to lose her job. She should remember that she can only control what she says and does, but she can't control her boss's actions. Jody should tell her boss that his comments and suggestions make her feel uncomfortable and she wants him to stop. Confronting her boss will take courage, and in certain situations, can be impracticable. But accepting the reality that her boss is in the wrong will allow her to do her best to reach a resolution. She can also choose to report him to Human Resources or to the Equal Employment Opportunity Commission.

Standing up to her boss could cost Jody her job, and wrongful termination appeals are not always successful. In that case, she will need to rely on her acceptance skills, mourn the loss of her job, and let things be as they are. No matter the outcome, the most important thing is that she has maintained her integrity. She hasn't compromised herself or allowed herself to be manipulated, used, and violated by her boss.

UNFAIR EVALUATIONS

Zen Maxims: Breathe/Be Mindful; Be Present/Connect; Accept Reality; Don't Be Self-Centered; Do Your Best/Let Go; Respect/Honor All Beings

The Problem: Josh just received his annual written evaluation from his supervisor. He feels that he performed excellently, completing his assignments on time, decreasing costs, and increasing sales and profits. However, his supervisor has rated him a three on a five-point scale, commenting that Josh "lacked initiative and commitment."

The Zen Approach: Josh feels that he's been rated unfairly and would like to arrange a meeting to speak with his supervisor. Before their meeting, he should take a few mindful breaths and remember to present his case in a professional manner. He shouldn't barge in and accuse his boss of being biased and unfair. Instead, he should present his argument supporting his excellent work, and then ask his boss to explain what "lacking initiative and commitment" specifically means and what he needs to do to earn a higher rating. Josh should be calm and centered, receiving what his boss says without rejecting it offhand or acting defensive and argumentative. Josh should allow himself time to contemplate the boss's perspective and consider whether it is valid. No one likes negative feedback, but there is often room for improvement, and it's sometimes difficult to clearly perceive our own flaws and deficiencies.

Josh can now plot his course. Should he work at impressing his boss by improving his performance in the areas the boss specified, write a memo to the boss providing evidence of why the boss's judgment is wrong, or shrug it off and let things be? Josh can make that choice taking all perspectives into account and not out of ego-based, reactive anger.

THE INCOMPETENT TEAM MEMBER

Zen Maxims: Breathe/Be Mindful; Be Present/Connect; Accept Reality; Don't Believe All Your Thoughts; Do Your Best/Let Go

The Problem: Sandra excels at her position as a nurse in a nursing home, but she often feels unable to effectively care for her patients because the physician who writes the medical orders makes poor decisions. Many of her patients are overmedicated, inadequately medicated, or their symptoms are being ignored. Whenever she suggests improvements to patient care, the physician sarcastically says, "Where did you get your license to practice medicine?"

The Zen Approach: Sandra's nursing license obligates her not to follow bad medical orders, but she's also not permitted to write her own and is therefore dependent on the physician's directives. Sandra needs to document his medical errors and his responses to her suggestions, then bring her complaints up the chain of command to the Director of Nursing. Maybe the nursing home administration will counsel him to improve or replace him with a new physician, but it's also possible it will fail to act at all.

Sandra must be prepared for all three alternatives. This means being mindfully aware of what her responsible choices are and what she's willing to tolerate. Quitting and looking for a new position is an option but leaves the patients in the doctor's care at risk. Going outside the chain of command to complain to the local medical society puts her at risk of being blackballed. Staying in her role and continuing to dispute orders is also an option but requires considerable mindfulness as she manages the day-by-day stress of the situation. She would need to allow her anger-producing thoughts—"How dare he speak to me that way; I can't believe he treats these patients so poorly!"—to come and go without getting attached to them. Instead, she should just focus on doing her job correctly, documenting the doctor's mistakes, and taking satisfaction in protecting vulnerable patients as best she can.

OVERLOOKED FOR PROMOTION

Zen Maxims: Breathe/Be Mindful; Be Present/Connect; Don't Believe All Your Thoughts; Don't Be Self-Centered; Do Your Best/Let Go

The Problem: Gary has worked at his firm for five years and has seen many coworkers promoted while he's always passed over. Gary believes that his promoted colleagues had no more seniority than he and were no better at their jobs.

The Zen Approach: Gary wonders why this keeps happening. Is there a problem with his performance? Is he being discriminated against? Are his promoted coworkers benefiting from personal connections? Rather than spinning his wheels and imagining all sorts of reasons, Gary should act and find out. He should arrange a meeting with his boss to ask why we hasn't been promoted and whether he has a future with the company.

Perhaps there are logical reasons for Gary's lack of a promotion. Maybe his coworkers had special backgrounds or areas of expertise that suited them for their new positions. It's also possible that Gary's boss wants him to improve in certain areas or develop new skills before he's eligible for promotion. Conversely, his boss may just not view him as promotion material. Whatever the outcome of the meeting, it will give Gary the information to understand his future at the firm—to accept staying in place, develop new skills or apply to another company.

Zen teaches us that the emotional drama of anger and self-pity this situation evokes is strictly optional. Instead, we should just understand the reality of the situation we are in and respond to it effectively by doing whatever it calls for. Zen tells us to do this over and over again, moment after moment. Sometimes we are unclear about what a situation requires. When this happens, we should meditate amid our confusion, watching our thoughts and feelings come and go, until clarity emerges.

TOO MUCH PAPERWORK

Zen Maxims: Accept Reality; Don't Believe All Your Thoughts; Don't Be Self-Centered; Do Your Best/Let Go; Be Upright/Maintain Integrity

The Problem: Angela feels like she spends more time documenting her work than working. She feels she would be much more productive if she could focus on her "real job." Her inbox is filled with incomplete forms her boss is demanding she hand in—but she no longer remembers all the information she needs to complete them. "Oh, well," she concludes. "I'll just fill in the blanks with whatever."

The Zen Approach: Although Angela would be able to complete more of her other work if she skipped the documentation, her company thinks the documentation *is* an important part of her job. Documentation may be required for reimbursement, for providing vital decision-making information, or protection against litigation. Angela needs to stop believing that documentation isn't part of her real job.

She also must change her behavior, allotting enough time each day for completing paperwork. She should also rethink her plan to randomly fill in missing data. That may conceal her negligence, but it also creates a liability for her should those forms be reviewed by an oversight agency or become evidence in a lawsuit. It would be more honest and courageous to admit that she's fallen behind in her paperwork and ask her boss's guidance and forgiveness. Maybe he'll just issue a warning, or maybe he'll terminate her. Zen teaches that accepting our karma and maintaining our integrity are crucial aspects of the path to spiritual maturity.

TIME TO MOVE ON?

Zen Maxims: Breathe/Be Mindful; Don't Believe All Your Thoughts; Do What's Needed; Do Your Best/Let Go

The Problem: Emily has reached the top of her pay grade, and there are no openings for advancement at her firm. She knows the only way to earn more is to move on, but she's comfortable in her current position and it's been a long time since she had to apply and interview for jobs. She's a shy person and knows that she doesn't come across well in stressful interviews.

The Zen Approach: Emily needs to sit with her uncertainty until she gains some clarity. Meditating and mindful awareness of all her conflicting thoughts and feelings is the first step. She can then accept all her feelings about leaving, pro and con, and hold them in a larger space of equanimity and "not knowing." As she allows things to settle, she will gradually discern her real priorities. Is a bigger salary worth giving up a congenial work environment? Is she more motivated by her comfort with her present work or by her discomfort with interviewing?

If Emily decides it's worth looking for a job that pays more, the next step is to deal with the thoughts that prevent her from interviewing well. Zen teaches that it is better to face things than avoid them. It's the way we develop courage and overcome fear. Old habitual, reactive thoughts may appear, related to feelings of inferiority, catastrophizing over possible failure—"It would be terrible if I didn't do well on this interview"—or fears of not being seen as perfect. Working on these thoughts means learning not to believe them when they occur. No one is perfect, and failure in an interview isn't a life-changing catastrophe. The more Emily can stop believing her thoughts, the easier interviewing will become, and the odds of an interview being successful will increase.

FAMILY MEDICAL LEAVE

Zen Maxims: Breathe/Be Mindful; Be Present/Connect; Do What's Needed; Do Your Best/Let Go; Respect/Honor All Beings; Be Upright/Maintain Integrity

The Problem: Tim's father lives by himself in another town. He's recently suffered a stroke and is still in an acute-care hospital. Tim doesn't know how much his father will recover or whether he can return to independent living, so he would like to take time off from work to tend to his father's needs. Tim's company offers family medical leave, but it's crunch time at work, and he is unsure how taking time off may affect his job security.

The Zen Approach: Tim should begin by talking to his boss to get a clearer idea of the risk of taking time off now. If the boss can reassure him they'll keep his position open without penalty, the choice becomes easy. If the boss's answer is more ambiguous, Tim needs to meditate, allowing full awareness of his conflicting feelings about helping his father and risking his job. If he sits with these feelings, allowing them to be as they are without adding emotions like guilt or shame, he will gradually gain some clarity about his decision.

Maybe there are other family members who can help, and Tim's presence isn't essential right now. Maybe Tim is his father's only support, and if he doesn't step in, his father will suffer greatly. Zen's emphasis on being kind, upright, and respecting and honoring all beings may incline him to help his ill father, but Tim must also be kind to himself. What if losing this job left Tim without the money to care for his father, or resulted in his homelessness, or in losing the health insurance he needs to take care of a chronic illness?

There's no crystal ball that can guarantee us the results of our decisions will turn out to be the best. In the end, Tim can only make the best decision he can amid many uncertainties. He should do his best, and then let go.

AM I GOOD ENOUGH?

Zen Maxims: Breathe/Be Mindful; Don't Believe All Your Thoughts;
Do Your Best/Let Go

The Problem: Monica has just been promoted to executive vice
president, with the responsibility of getting an important new project
off the ground. While she was good at her previous job, she's unsure
of her ability to handle the increased responsibilities. The pace of
decision making and the costs of making mistakes have both risen.
"What if I'm not good enough for this job?" she wonders.

The Zen Approach: It does no good to wonder. Either Monica's
good enough, she'll learn how to be good enough, or she'll fail.
Her mistake is tying her competence at her new job to her worth
as a human being. She's still Monica, a human being fully worthy
of self-esteem and respect, whether she's successful at the job or
not. Rather than worrying about her self-worth, she should focus on
her job performance and doing the best she can. All these thoughts
about her adequacy only interfere with her performance. In her meditation, Monica can observe thoughts about her competence come
and go without attaching to them or pushing them away. When she
becomes deeply familiar with them, she can begin observing them
with a sense of humor: "Here, you are again, my dear old familiar
thoughts of self-doubt."

WRITER'S BLOCK

Breathe/Be Mindful; Don't Believe All Your Thoughts; Do Your Best/Let Go

The Problem: Madison has a term paper due soon but can't seem to get started. An idea for the paper just won't come.

The Zen Approach: Creativity is often blocked by an inner critical voice that cripples us before we can even begin. This inner voice criticizes any idea we come up with as not being good enough, so we hesitate to even commit it to paper. We can't always turn off our inner critic, but we can become familiar with it through mindfully observing our thoughts, accustomed enough that we learn to treat it like a familiar old friend who can be relegated to the corner and ignored. Then the trick is: Just write. Just do it. Set yourself the task of putting a paragraph or two on paper, typing the first thing that comes to mind. You can't write (a creative act) and edit (a critical act) at the same time. Whatever you write may turn out to be drivel, but don't worry about that. You can edit it or toss it later. At least you now have your juices flowing. The rest will come.

LAID OFF

Zen Maxims: Accept Reality; Don't Believe All Your Thoughts; Do Your Best/Let Go

The Problem: Scott has been laid off after 15 years at his company, and at age 55, he's still a long way from retirement age. There aren't other jobs in his town that call for his experience and expertise or offer a commensurate salary, and he hates the idea of uprooting his family. He thinks to himself, "Who will want to hire someone my age, anyway?"

The Zen Approach: Scott is in danger of being hampered by his own negative thinking. Yes, it's harder to find a job at age 55, jobs in his town are scarce, and he doesn't like the idea of moving, but these are all limiting thoughts, discouraging him before he even gets started. Unlike his thoughts, his specific future is unwritten. Sometimes older people are hired for jobs and age is a nonfactor. A new job may even become available in his town. It's possible he might have to move, as a last resort, which would be a major hassle and disruption, but not the worst-case scenario. Who knows, the new community he moves to might be even nicer than his beloved old community.

Scott must do his best to find a new position without burdening himself with all the what-ifs. He can put the word out to acquaintances in his field both locally and in other communities and learn about new digital job search resources that weren't available when he was last on the job market. He should keep in mind that his vast experience in his field may be valued by a potential employer. He may have to adjust to a lower salary, which may be a major hassle and disruption, but very few people's lives go exactly as planned. Even if he must sacrifice a part of his dreams, his life may still be vastly better than innumerable others who get by with less and endure greater hardships. Zen teaches that accepting reality means learning to put our losses in perspective and being grateful for what we still have.

WHISTLEBLOWER

Zen Maxims: Breathe/Be Mindful; Be Kind; Do What's Needed; Respect/Honor All Beings; Be Upright/Maintain Integrity

The Problem: George discovered a female coworker is having a sexual relationship with a male supervisor, which is a clear violation of company policy. George considers whether he should report it or keep it to himself.

The Zen Approach: Some people hold themselves and others rigidly accountable for even small violations of behavioral rules. They are busybodies who need to report every infraction and see all transgressors severely punished. This is one sure way not to get along with people.

On the other hand, many workers, especially women, are psychologically traumatized by office predators who try to coerce them into having sexual relations. The company has good reasons for forbidding personal relationships between employees.

George doesn't want to stir up office hostilities, but he also doesn't want to stand by while someone is harmed. The first thing he should do is be mindfully aware of all the different factors. This includes his past assessments of the supervisor's character and the supervisee's vulnerability, his awareness of office politics and the likely repercussions of reporting the affair, and his insight into his own motives. Is he motivated by compassion for the supervisee, or by self-righteousness, ambition, or petty vindictiveness?

If after contemplating all these factors he decides he must act, he should have a private conversation with the supervisee. He should tell her that he's aware of the affair and ask whether it's a consensual relationship or if she feels intimidated or coerced. If it's consensual, George should just butt out. Yes, they're violating company policy, but that is no longer any of his business.

If she's being abused, George should discuss reporting the situation to Human Resources with her and see how she responds. Maybe she'll prefer handling things herself and doesn't want his meddling or perhaps she'll be grateful for his intervention. Whatever George finally decides to do, his intention should be, first and foremost, to minimize harm to the supervisee.

Chapter Five

ZEN ON THE GO

Our lives are not limited to home or work. Not only do we travel between home and work, but we go on business trips and vacations, travel to visit friends and family, and tour the world to broaden our horizons. While modern transportation is one of the greatest miracles of our age, it can also be the source of some of our worst headaches. Lengthy commutes, traffic jams and accidents, road rage, jet lag, airport delays, and lost baggage are just some of the challenges we face on a daily basis.

Whatever the problem, Zen is ready to come to our rescue, enabling us to handle difficulties with wisdom and equanimity. Once again, we only have to remember our Zen Maxims: 1) Breathe/Be Mindful, 2) Be Present and Connect, 3) Accept Reality As It Is, 4) Be Kind to Yourself and Others, 5) Don't Believe All Your Thoughts, 6) Don't Be Overly Self-Centered, 7) Do What's Needed, 8) Do Your Best, Then Let Go, 9) Respect and Honor All Beings, and 10) Be Upright/Maintain Integrity.

STUCK IN TRAFFIC

Zen Maxims: Breathe/Be Mindful; Be Present/Connect; Accept Reality; Don't Believe All Your Thoughts; Do Your Best/Let Go

The Problem: Samantha is going nowhere fast in bumper-to-bumper traffic on the interstate. Her GPS shows an accident five miles ahead, and there are no off-ramps between here and there. At this rate, it will be hours before she reaches her destination.

The Zen Approach: Anger and frustration will do nothing to get Samantha to where she needs to go any faster and will just make her time sitting in traffic more painful. Samantha should take a mindful breath, accept the reality of the situation, and then just let go. She can use the flashing red lights of the taillights in front of her as mindfulness reminders. Whenever she sees a taillight flash red, she can take another mindful breath and let go a little more. Whenever she has the thought "It will be terrible if I'm late," she should let the thought go without believing in it. It will be unfortunate if she's late, but unless she's a surgeon heading to an emergency operation, it will hardly be a catastrophe. Most things can be missed, delayed, or rescheduled if necessary. Samantha should call ahead, let people know she'll be unavoidably late, put on the radio, and enjoy the music as she sits there.

FENDER BENDER

Zen Maxims: Breathe/Be Mindful; Accept Reality; Don't Believe All Your Thoughts; Do What's Needed; Do Your Best/Let Go; Respect/Honor All Beings

The Problem: Erik just bought the new car last month, and now it has its first dent. He was stopped at a red light when someone hit him from the rear. He fumes behind the wheel as he waits for the police to arrive.

The Zen Approach: When a new car gets its first dent, we can feel like we ourselves have been injured, but Zen teaches us that everything is impermanent, and nothing stays in pristine shape forever. It's inevitable that despite our best efforts, parts wear out and need replacement, and scrapes, dents, and dings come with the mileage. The newness of the car makes it especially painful. We knew something like this would happen sometime, but did it *have* to be so soon? That thought makes us fume.

The reality is, it *did* have to happen so soon given the presence of a careless driver on the road who wasn't looking where he was going. The newness of Erik's car was irrelevant to the universe. He should take a few mindful breaths, breathing in acceptance with each in-breath, and letting go with each out-breath. Getting angry doesn't make the dent go away. Erik should focus on being effective and doing what needs to be done instead. He should get the other driver's license and insurance information and wait for the police to arrive.

There's no need to get into an argument or fight with the person who hit his car. What's done is done. The other person might have been stupid, incompetent, overtired, or intoxicated, but yelling at him won't change any of that. Erik should honor and respect the humanity of the person who hit his car and do his best to remain civil.

ROAD RAGE

Zen Maxims: Breathe/Be Mindful; Accept Reality; Be Kind; Don't Believe All Your Thoughts; Respect/Honor All Beings

The Problem: Ryan hit his brakes when another car cut into his lane, pulling in front of him at an unsafe distance. His first impulse is to pull alongside the other car to give the driver a piece of his mind.

The Zen Approach: A Zen master once said this about anger: If this was the last five minutes of your life, would you want to spend it being this angry? If the answer is "yes," go ahead; otherwise, let it go.

If Ryan feels the need to let the other driver know his poor driving could have caused an accident, beeping his horn is sufficient. The driver will get the point, so why pull up ahead and start a fight? In truth, getting angry will do nothing to improve the situation. The other driver may feel intimidated, or feel a need to retaliate in kind, but he won't become a better driver because Ryan confronts him.

Ryan should just take a couple of mindful breaths, cool down, and consider trying some other attitudes. Is it possible for him to feel grateful he avoided an accident? Is it possible for him to mentally practice sending good wishes to the careless driver, wishes that he successfully overcomes being aggressive, overtired, or drunk? Wishes like these do nothing to improve the other driver, but they can go a long way toward improving us.

AIRPORT DELAY

Zen Maxims: Breathe/Be Mindful; Accept Reality; Don't Be Self-Centered; Do What's Needed; Do Your Best/Let Go

The Problem: Kathleen is waiting to board the red-eye to Denver for a morning business meeting when she gets word that weather conditions have occasioned a delay. No one can say when the flight will take off or whether it might even be canceled. The business meeting is not one she can afford to miss.

The Zen Approach: If there is no way Kathleen can get to Denver on time, she needs to practice radical acceptance: this *is* the way it is. She should mindfully breathe in acceptance, and mindfully breathe out letting go. She may be troubled by the thought "But I have to get there on time," but she should just let that thought go. She would very much like to be in Denver on time, but there's no reason why the universe *has* to cooperate with her wish. It does its own thing. To think that the universe ought to comply with her wishes is being self-centered. The only thing she needs to do is contact the people she was going to meet with in Denver, and either offer to reschedule the meeting or arrange to attend via videoconferencing.

LOST LUGGAGE

Zen Maxims: Breathe/Be Mindful; Accept Reality; Be Kind;
Do What's Needed

The Problem: Kelly made it to London, but her luggage didn't. The
airline says it might be a day or two before they can locate it and get
it to her hotel. She has tickets to a concert that night and nothing
appropriate to wear.

The Zen Approach: Kelly can choose to get very upset over her
delayed luggage, but that doesn't get her luggage to her any sooner.
She can yell at the baggage claim personnel, but they weren't
the ones who lost it. She should breathe mindfully and accept the
situation as it is. It's an inconvenience, but not a catastrophe. Maybe
there's time to go shopping before the concert tonight and pick up
something nice to wear. If Kelly was wise enough to take out trip
insurance, she can pay for the new clothes through her insurance
reimbursement.

OVERSEAS VACATION

Zen Maxims: Breathe/Be Mindful; Don't Believe All Your Thoughts; Do Your Best/Let Go

The Problem: Brittany is planning a dream trip to Paris, her first vacation overseas. She is overwhelmed by all the decisions: how to buy the cheapest airline tickets; where to stay; how to travel from the airport to her hotel; what to see; where to eat; and whether to buy trip insurance. She wants this vacation to be great and keeps spinning her wheels.

The Zen Approach: Brittany believes that every choice she makes must be perfect. She thinks it would be awful if she booked the second cheapest flight, stayed at the second-best hotel, dined in the third-best restaurant, and didn't see every sight. In fact, there is no such thing as "the perfect trip," but there are many possible "good enough" trips. Brittany will disappoint herself if she compares every experience she has in Paris to some imagined ideal. She will look out from the Eiffel Tower and be disappointed if it's a cloudy day. She will order the onion soup at a fancy restaurant and be disappointed if it's not all that different from the onion soup back home.

Brittany would make things easier on herself if she just made the best choices she can without second-guessing herself every step of the way. If she can't decide which of two hotels is better, both are probably fine. She should choose one and get on with it. If she finds an acceptable airfare, just book it. Maybe it would be cheaper if she bought it later in the week, but that's life. The Zen way is to do your best in each moment, then let go. No matter how you try, you will never do things perfectly, but you can always do things well enough.

BATHING SUIT

Zen Maxims: Breathe/Be Mindful; Accept Reality; Be Kind; Don't Believe All Your Thoughts; Do Your Best/Let Go

The Problem: Danielle is on vacation with friends in a sunny beach town. She bought a new bathing suit for the occasion, but subsequently put on a few pounds. She eyes herself in the mirror as she tries it on. Maybe she won't go to the beach with her friends and will just stay in and read a book.

The Zen Approach: It's sad that Danielle is letting her critical self-consciousness deter her from enjoying the surf and sand. The ocean and beach don't care if she's overweight or doesn't look her best. What's stopping Danielle are her own self-critical thoughts: "It would be terrible if others think I'm fat" or "I couldn't stand my friends seeing me not looking my best."

While Danielle would prefer that others always view her noncritically, the reality is that others make judgments about us all the time, and at least some of those are bound to be critical. If we had to live our lives to avoid all critical judgments, none of us would ever go outside. Even the most divine human being sometimes has a hair out of place. We all make mistakes, act foolishly, or say things that don't come out quite right. Those who notice our imperfections forgive us for them because they love us or tick little boxes of disapproval and move on. Accepting reality means accepting the possibility of having one's imperfections noticed with a certain degree of equanimity and having the courage to live one's life fully regardless.

"Being perfect" usually means trying to live up to whatever irrational standards of perfection are the fashion of the day. This year ultra-thinness is in vogue; in the past curves were to be admired. The belief that we ought to be perfect is a source of untold suffering and misery. How much better to accept the inevitability of our imperfections, do our best, and let go.

DINING ALONE

Zen Maxims: Breathe/Be Mindful; Don't Believe All Your Thoughts; Do Your Best/Let Go

The Problem: Julie is staying in a hotel on a business trip to a new city. She is trying to decide whether to get room service or dine out in the hotel's fancy restaurant. She's never dined out alone before and wonders how awkward it might feel. She thinks she might feel terribly alone just sitting by herself.

The Zen Approach: In reality, Julie is no more alone in the restaurant than she is in her hotel room. If she *feels* more alone in the restaurant, it is because of her self-pitying thoughts—"How sad that I'm all alone here while everyone else seems to have a companion." Maybe she worries about how others will evaluate her—"What must everyone else in the restaurant think of me?" If she could allow these thoughts to come and go without becoming attached to them, she could focus instead on how her meal tastes.

The reality is that others are probably enjoying their meals without giving Julie much thought. While she would prefer having company, it doesn't say anything negative about her that she doesn't have any friends in this new town. While she might enjoy her meal more if she ate with a friend, she can still enjoy the meal itself. In fact, without the distraction of conversation, she might be able to mindfully savor the tastes of her meal in a more rich and intense way than she normally would. Who knows? This could be the most delicious meal of her life.

BAD WEATHER

Zen Maxims: Accept Reality; Do Your Best/Let Go

The Problem: Matt and Pam laid out a fortune for their Hawaiian honeymoon, but now that they're in Honolulu, it's raining every day. Matt can't help feeling cheated and disappointed.

The Zen Approach: Matt has a choice. He can keep comparing the present moment with some imagined perfect moment, or he can accept the moment as it is. This means letting go of his fantasies about how things ought to be and appreciating what's actually happening. If Matt can get in touch with the present moment, he'll see that he and his lovely new bride are comfortably ensconced in a beautiful hotel one thousand miles from the tensions of everyday life. They are free to enjoy intimacy, watch the latest movies on their large screen TV, or order in from room service. Later they can try the lounge to enjoy drinks with little umbrellas and take in the slack-string guitar concert, the hula dancers, or whatever other entertainment is on offer. It's a shame Matt and Pam haven't been swimming at Waikiki yet, but they don't have to let that make them utterly miserable.

LOST

Zen Maxims: Breathe/Be Mindful; Do What's Needed

The Problem: Ron has driven around in circles for the past ten minutes trying to find the odd little side street where the restaurant is located. Jessica suggests they stop and ask someone, but Ron is sure he'll find it if he just keeps circling.

The Zen Approach: Why does Ron find it hard to stop and ask for directions? Does he need to prove he can do everything by himself? Is he afraid of appearing less than competent in front of Jessica? Is he stubbornly resistant to taking suggestions? Is he anxious about accosting strangers? Whatever the reason, Ron is allowing an irrelevant need or fear get in the way of successfully getting to the restaurant on time.

Ron's immediate impulse is to ignore Jessica's suggestion and keep circling, hoping for a stroke of luck. Rather than following that automatic impulse, Ron should take a breath and consider what Jessica says. As he breathes, he can ask himself, "Why am I being so resistant?"

He doesn't necessarily need to figure out the answer. Zen counsels us to sit with questions and allow them to percolate. Just pausing to ask the question acts as a circuit breaker interrupting our habitual patterns of response and creating a space in which we can choose to act differently.

DIETARY RESTRICTIONS

Zen Maxims: Do What's Needed; Do Your Best/Let Go; Respect/Honor All Beings

The Problem: Friends have asked Jackie if she wants to eat out with them after the movie. Jackie is on a special diet because of health concerns, and there are very few foods she can safely eat. The usual haunts where her friends eat are not good for her, but she doesn't want to be a "downer," dragging them someplace where they'll be unhappy. She wonders if she should decline their invitation.

The Zen Approach: It's good that Jackie wants to eat healthily and is concerned about her friends' happiness. On the other hand, Jackie's friends have invited her and would clearly enjoy her company. Her worry that they'll not be able to find a mutually agreeable restaurant may be overblown. She shouldn't let it prevent her from trying. How could it hurt to make the attempt?

Jackie doesn't want to be like some people she knows who are overly picky about food preferences and dictate them to others, but she doesn't have to present herself that way. There's a way to balance her health needs with concerns for her friends' happiness. Jackie could tell her friends, "I'd love to join you, but I have some health needs and I'd hate to spoil your evening by making you go to a restaurant you wouldn't enjoy. If we can find a restaurant we all can enjoy, great. If not, maybe we can find some other way to get together." We are at our best when we are upfront, honest, and kind.

JET LAG

Zen Maxims: Breathe/Be Mindful; Accept Reality; Do What's Needed

The Problem: Carole planned to hit the ground running when she landed in Paris, but she couldn't sleep on the plane and now she finds herself out of energy. She has a big day planned, but all she wants to do is nap.

The Zen Approach: Carole has her itinerary all worked out in her head, but her body is telling her otherwise. Zen teaches us to be good listeners—to "listen within" to our minds, hearts, and bodies to better discern our genuine needs in each moment. If Carole mindfully reflected on the question "What do I really need right now?" she would wisely choose to catch up on her sleep, even if it meant missing some Parisian attractions. She'd be doing herself no favor if she depleted herself further, dragging her unwilling body through the Louvre. Better to rest now so that she stays well, regains her energy, and can fully enjoy the rest of her trip.

LANGUAGE BARRIER

Zen Maxims: Breathe/Be Mindful; Do What's Needed

The Problem: Craig is traveling by train from Seville to Granada when the conductor examines his ticket, frowns, mutters something in Spanish that Craig can't understand, and moves on. There seems to be a problem, but Craig can't figure out what it is.

When things like this happen, Craig feels close to panicking. He wonders, "What if I'm on the wrong train, or if I have to get off this train and transfer to another?" The conductor doesn't speak English and can't help.

The Zen Approach: The first thing Craig should do is take a few mindful breaths and calm down. Whatever the problem is, it won't prove fatal. Any mistake he may have made can eventually be corrected, even if it creates a delay or inconvenience. It helps to keep things in perspective.

What Craig needs is someone who understands English and Spanish. Maybe some other passenger in the car is bilingual? Ordinarily, Craig doesn't like to accost strangers; it makes him feel uncomfortable. This situation, however, calls on him to overcome his discomfort and focus on doing what's needed. Craig should stand up and address the fellow passengers in his car: "Excuse me, does anyone speak English?" If no one does, he can try the next car. Chances are, he will eventually find someone who can read his ticket and explain the problem to him.

WHEN IN JERUSALEM

Zen Maxims: Breathe/Be Mindful; Don't Believe All Your Thoughts; Don't Be Self-Centered; Respect/Honor All Beings

The Problem: Leah is looking forward to sightseeing Jerusalem's old city wearing her go-to summertime outfit of a halter top and cut-offs. Her Israeli tour guide says she's dressed inappropriately and must change into clothes that completely cover her arms and legs. Leah feels offended. Where does he get off telling her how to dress?

The Zen Approach: At home Leah's entitled to dress how she likes, but now she's another country's guest. While she's entitled to her own opinions, guests should be sensitive, whenever possible, to their host's customs, rules, and points of view. Leah should take a few mindful breaths and realize she has little to lose by accommodating her host's wishes. It's not as if they're requiring her to do something dangerous, immoral, or illegal. Surely she can suspend her own desires to honor and respect her host's sensitivities.

Leah may be thinking, "The way I dress is an expression of my identity, and I must be completely free to express my identity everywhere and at all times." She should be aware that thinking this way doesn't make it true. The way Leah dresses only superficially reflects her identity—it doesn't define who she authentically is. There is also no law of the universe that says she must always be free to do as she wants. Lasting happiness comes from finding the right balance between expressing our individuality and living in harmony with others—not from doing whatever we please.

DECLINED CREDIT CARD

Zen Maxims: Breathe/Be Mindful; Don't Believe All Your Thoughts;
Do What's Needed

The Problem: Olivia is paying for a purchase at an airport gift shop
when the check-out person says her credit card has been declined.
She feels embarrassed—does the cashier think she's trying to pull a
fast one? She's also worried. Did some scammer run up fraudulent
purchases on her account? Is her credit ruined?

The Zen Approach: Credit cards can be declined for benign reasons, but Olivia's mind is already jumping to worst-case scenarios.
She has no real evidence that the check-out person thinks any the
worse of her and no reason to suspect her credit is ruined. Olivia
should take a few mindful breaths and recognize that her thoughts
are not reality. Then she can then stop rehearsing the fear-inducing
thoughts, calm down, and focus on devising an effective action plan.

Olivia should call her credit card company and see where the
problem lies. Credit card purchases are sometimes declined to
protect the owner from potential fraud. This is especially true if
Olivia failed to notify the credit card company she would be traveling abroad. A simple phone call is often all it takes to clear up any
misunderstanding.

I'LL NEVER FORGET WHAT'S-HIS-NAME

Zen Maxims: Be Present/Connect; Be Kind; Do Your Best/Let Go; Be Upright/Maintain Integrity

The Problem: Bruce is attending a convention in Las Vegas. A man with a vaguely familiar face begins pumping his arm. "Bruce, old boy! Long time no see!" Bruce has no idea who the man is but feels embarrassed to admit it.

The Zen Approach: Bruce has to decide whether to pretend to recognize the man or confess his ignorance. He could say something vague like "Good to see you too! How's it going?" and hope the man's reply may provide some clue to his identity. If they can keep the conversation at the level of a brief superficial greeting, Bruce may never have to admit his ignorance.

On the other hand, if Bruce decides to be honest, he can begin with a brief apology: "I'm sorry, this is embarrassing, but for the moment I can't recall how I know you." This may hurt his greeter's feelings, but it puts the encounter on a more authentic basis. The man can now remind Bruce who he is and what their past acquaintance has been, and a real conversation becomes possible. Perhaps something valuable may come from this encounter despite the initial discomfort.

From a Zen perspective, the important question is, who exactly is Bruce protecting if he pretends to recognize the man? Is he protecting himself from embarrassment, or the other person from hurt feelings? Zen would say if his primary goal is to avoid embarrassment, he should overcome his fear and risk being genuine. We should never be afraid to present ourselves as the fallible beings we are. What a relief to accept ourselves as we are, without needing to always project an image of perfection. On the other hand, if Bruce's primary goal is to spare the other's feelings, this is in accord with the Zen maxim of kindness to all beings. In Zen, our motivation makes a difference. Acting from fear diminishes us, acting with compassion enlarges us.

THE PHANTOM SEAT

Zen Maxims: Be Present/Connect; Do What's Needed; Do Your Best/Let Go

The Problem: Hank boards the commuter rail during rush hour. All the seats are taken, except for a seat that contains a passenger's backpack. Hank tries to make eye contact with the passenger, but the passenger ignores him.

The Zen Approach: Hank is so uncomfortable asserting himself that he'd rather stand for an hour until the train reaches the terminal than ask a stranger to do him a favor. And why should that be? The passenger with the backpack paid for one seat but is occupying two, while Hank paid for a seat, but doesn't have any. He has every right to ask the passenger to make room for him.

Zen would say that Hank should take a few mindful breaths and meditate on his resistance to doing what the situation calls for. What's the worst that could happen? Is Hank afraid the passenger will look disgruntled and refuse his request? If it happened, Hank could always complain to the conductor, or he could choose to accept the situation without further escalation.

Hank's reluctance reflects his general passive-submissive attitude—an attitude that probably hampers his ability to be successful in other areas of his life as well. This situation offers Hank a perfect opportunity to practice overcoming this self-defeating attitude. Zen says that we can view every difficulty in our lives as an opportunity for practice.

MISSED CONNECTIONS

Zen Maxims: Breathe/Be Mindful; Accept Reality; Do Your Best/Let Go

The Problem: The first leg of Lynn's flight out of New York was delayed, and she missed her connecting flight from Amsterdam to Rome. The next available connecting flight isn't until tomorrow. She's furious.

The Zen Approach: Lynn can choose how she's going to spend her day in Amsterdam. She can spend the time complaining and making herself miserable, or she can take a few mindful breaths, drop the moaning and groaning, and let go and enjoy her day as best she can.

Amsterdam's Schiphol airport has many restaurants and shops, and Amsterdam is a first-rate tourist destination. The airline may provide her with overnight lodging, and if Lynn has taken out trip insurance, she'll be reimbursed a modest sum for the delay. Time to relax and see the sights: the Van Gogh Museum, anyone? Rome can wait until tomorrow.

Zen says that we always have a choice about how we view our difficulties. If a problem can be solved, why be upset about it? If a problem can't be fixed, why waste energy fretting? Focus on doing what you can and let go of the rest. A certain amount of irritation is a natural response to being forced to change plans, but staying upset is purely optional.

PHOBIA

Zen Maxims: Breathe/Be Mindful; Don't Believe All Your Thoughts; Do What's Needed

The Problem: Ever since Luke had a panic attack while crossing a bridge, he's avoided crossing bridges. Commuting to his new job requires him to cross a bridge five days a week. He wakes up each morning in a cold sweat just thinking about it. Did he make a mistake taking the new job?

The Zen Approach: Luke can use Zen meditation to both reduce his anxiety and become more aware of how his thoughts create his anxiety. Mindful breathing works because it is inherently relaxing, and because focusing on our breathing prevents us from focusing on our anxiety-producing thoughts. When anxiety-provoking thoughts intrude, however, its useful to see them as objects of thought and not as reflections of reality.

Thoughts creating Luke's anxiety are related to loss of control and helplessness. He may be thinking, "What if the bridge collapsed while I was on it, trapped inside my car?" It's possible for bridges to collapse, but the odds of it happening while Luke is on one are exceedingly small.

Once Luke is able to, he needs to deliberately drive on the bridge over and over again. This takes an effort of will, but it is the only way to overcome fear. The more we avoid things, the more likely we are to avoid them again in the future. The more we confront our fears, the more likely we are to overcome them. Every wisdom tradition recognizes this. Aristotle recognized that we develop the virtue of courage through practice. Modern psychology calls this exposure therapy—we extinguish our fears by exposing ourselves to what we fear. In Zen, we simply say, "breathe," "your thoughts are not reality," and "do what's needed."

ROUNDABOUT ROUTE

Zen Maxims: Be Present/Connect; Do What's Needed; Do Your Best/ Let Go; Respect/Honor All Beings

The Problem: Lynn is taking a taxi from the airport to her hotel. She's familiar with the route from previous trips, and it seems like the driver is taking a roundabout route to jack up the fare.

The Zen Approach: Lynn must decide whether to say something or remain silent. She may be reluctant to speak up because she's unsure about her concerns or because she's fearful of confrontation. She shouldn't let her uncertainty or fear prevent her from communicating what's on her mind, however. Zen advises us to connect with others rather than avoiding contact, and to do what's needed.

Lynn doesn't have to open with an accusation that she's being cheated. She can begin by simply stating her observation that they're on a different route than usual, and "wouldn't it be quicker if we took the parkway?" The cabdriver might be able justify the new route ("the parkway's under construction," "there's been an accident") in a way that allays her concerns. If she's still doubtful, she can insist the driver turn around and take her via the parkway or else she'll complain to the cab company. As the paying customer, she has the right to ask that he take her preferred route.

Zen views every encounter as an opportunity to practice being our best selves. From the Zen perspective, this means overcoming our fears so that we can do what's called for in every situation while respecting and honoring others in the process.

TRUST PROBLEM

Zen Maxims: Breathe/Be Mindful; Do What's Needed

The Problem: Nora's taken her car in for a routine oil change. The mechanic tells her that while her car may seem to be running fine now, it has several expensive issues that will cause problems down the road. Nora doesn't know a lot about cars and worries the mechanic is taking advantage of her ignorance.

The Zen Approach: How can Nora know whether she's being taken advantage of? Given her limited knowledge of cars, she has no way of being certain. Zen teaches us we should never be too sure of our opinions. One famous Zen koan states, "Not knowing is most intimate." It's okay not be such a big expert about things.

The real question is, how should we act in the face of uncertainty? The Zen answer is "be mindful" and "do what's needed." Being mindful in this situation means being aware of one's uncertainty and resisting acting on impulse. What's needed in this situation is more information—an independent expert opinion. Rather than agreeing to the expensive servicing or accusing the mechanic of cheating her, Nora should take her car to another mechanic and offer to pay, not to repair the car, but for a second opinion. Once she has a second opinion, it will be clearer what she needs to do.

RESTROOM

Zen Maxims: Breathe/Be Mindful; Don't Believe All Your Thoughts; Do What's Needed

The Problem: Kim is sightseeing in New Orleans. She didn't use the bathroom before leaving her hotel, and now she urgently needs one. She sees a restaurant nearby but is embarrassed to ask to use their restroom when she doesn't plan to eat there.

The Zen Approach: It's the restaurateur's right to allow or refuse her request, but Kim has an equal right to ask. What does Kim risk by asking? The worst he can do is say no and treat her unkindly. While it's never pleasant to be refused or looked at askance, it's hardly a catastrophe. The restaurateur's opinion of Kim doesn't have to affect her at all if she views it properly. He isn't an important person in her life, and he doesn't know enough about Kim to hold a worthwhile opinion about her.

What's holding Kim back is her habitual belief that it's terribly important for everyone to have a positive impression of her. This is of course, nonsense. While we would all prefer that everyone always think positively about us, it's unreasonable to live as if it's the end all and be all of life. Rejections, large and small, are an inevitable part of life, and we're better off when we learn to accept them in stride.

Zen would say Kim should take a mindful breath and ask herself, "What's really needed here?" She can remind herself that her negative thoughts are just imagined possibilities, whereas her need to relieve herself is real and urgent. She can also visualize herself being refused by a haughty restaurateur, yet remaining unbowed.

STREET BEGGAR

Zen Maxims: Breathe/Be Mindful; Be Present/Connect; Don't Be Self-Centered; Be Kind; Respect/Honor All Beings

The Problem: Whenever Owen is approached by a person asking for money in the street, he has mixed feelings. He wants to think of himself as a generous person but worries the person will use any money he gives for alcohol or drugs. He also can't possibly give to every homeless person he sees. There are just too many.

The Zen Approach: Owen is right. There are countless beggars on the city streets, and it's not in his power to help them all. On the other hand, not all of them are approaching him right now. Just this one. Can he give to this one? Will he still have carfare to get home if he does? What's stopping Owen from giving the man anything?

The problem is Owen sees the beggar as someone other than himself. Dressed in rags, he doesn't seem to be a member of Owen's tribe. Maybe he's addicted to heroin, or mentally ill, or a scam artist. Maybe he'll waste whatever Owen gives him on a bottle of wine. These thoughts are barriers to compassion.

The reality is, whatever the beggar's story, Owen's life is unimaginably better off than the beggar's. If worse came to worst and the beggar spent the money on wine, it wouldn't affect Owen one way or another. If Owen made simple eye contact, Owen could see the beggar as a fellow human being in dire straits.

Whenever members of the Zulu ethnic group meet one another, they greet each other with "*Sawubona*," meaning, "I see you"—I see your humanity and dignity. That is the spirit in which Owen should meet the beggar's gaze. Zen says every encounter is an opportunity for us to let go of our self-centeredness and expand our capacity for empathy and compassionate generosity. The Zen bodhisattva vows state, "Sentient beings are numberless. I vow to save them all."

Of course that's an impossible task. It's like trying to empty the ocean of water one teaspoonful at a time. All we can do is do our best, one encounter at a time. But each time we take our vows seriously, we make ourselves and the world infinitesimally better.

Will giving a beggar a few dollars end inequality and injustice? Not really. It won't even begin to make a dent in the systemic problems that lead to poverty. Owen shouldn't delude himself that his one-on-one acts of charity fulfill his obligation to heal the world. They did help this one person this one brief moment, however, and allowed Owen to experience a deeper sense of his own humanity. That's a start.

CONFLICTS OF INTEREST

Zen Maxims: Breathe/Be Mindful; Accept Reality; Be Kind; Don't Be Overly Self-Centered; Do What's Needed

The Problem: Ruth and Sharon are sisters traveling together in Europe. Ruth loves shopping and checking out the local bars. Sharon is more into art museums and classical music. Ruth doesn't like doing anything by herself, and wants Sharon to accompany her everywhere, but Sharon would like time by herself to enjoy the things she likes.

The Zen Approach: Sharon needs to find the right balance between fulfilling her own desires and satisfying Ruth's. Our Zen maxim "Be Kind" means be kind to yourself as well as others. Ruth may want Sharon to accompany her everywhere, but her desires shouldn't completely eclipse Sharon's. They are two separate individuals, and they don't need to be constantly joined at the hip.

Negotiating this new balance can be a delicate matter. While Sharon needs to stand up to Ruth's unreasonable expectations and assert her own independence, she doesn't need to be unkind. Ruth's need for Sharon's companionship reflects her own dependency, vulnerability, and insecurity. Rather than making any sudden changes, Sharon should mindfully and calmly discuss her own needs with Ruth and begin a gradual weaning process. Sharon may end up on the receiving end of Ruth's anger over the change in their relationship. This will require Sharon to remain mindful, accepting the anger as an inevitable part of change without losing her equanimity.

At the same time, Ruth must work at being a little less self-centered, and exercise her own acceptance skills. Things aren't going back to the way they were before. Despite her initial discomfort, this might end up being a good thing for Ruth as she learns how to stand on her own two feet.

PART THREE

ZEN FORWARD

The following chapter offers suggestions and resources to help you continue to develop your understanding of Zen and become more deeply familiar with its practice. Remember, studying Zen is more like learning how to ride a bicycle than it is learning how to understand a philosophy. You can't just read about it; you have to practice it.

Chapter Six

STAYING ZEN

Zen is an endless journey of continuous practice. In the beginning, it helps us clear our minds, stay in touch with our bodies, be more present, and live more wholeheartedly with integrity and compassion. Over time, the spiritual nature of the practice ripens as we more fully realize our deep interconnection with all beings and existence itself.

The Zen Commitment

Being a Zen practitioner means committing to doing zazen on a regular basis. It makes a big difference if your practice is regular—not sporadic or haphazard. If you've only been meditating once or twice a week, try sitting every day. If you've only been meditating for short periods of time, try extending your sittings to 20 to 30 minutes in length. If you already have a daily sitting practice, try attending a *zazenkai* (a one-day Zen meditation retreat) or a **sesshin** (an intensive three-to-seven day Zen meditation retreat) offered through a local Zen center.

Being a Zen practitioner also means making the commitment to view everything in one's life as practice—relationships with family, friends, and work; the way we clean, cook, shop, eat, spend, volunteer, and enjoy our leisure—and maintaining integrity and a compassionate heart in all one's interactions.

Zen calls us to be mindful every moment of our lives. Mindfulness helps us to savor the texture of each moment, to accept life and let go of our fixations, to avoid living in our thoughts and be fully alive, to have more meaningful relationships with others, and to be more open, direct, and generous. It also helps us focus on what really matters in our lives so that we can build lives truly worth living.

Zen Community

If you're serious about pursuing Zen, it helps to find a community of fellow practitioners. Zen is not a journey one can undertake alone. You will have many questions along the way, and a Zen teacher and a community of experienced practitioners is an invaluable resource that can help keep your practice from going astray.

A Zen community of practitioners is called a **sangha**. You may already know of a Zen sangha in or near your town, whether it be a sitting group, Zen center, or temple. If not, a simple internet search will reveal the closest ones. If there are several nearby, visit each of them to discover which one you feel most comfortable with.

You should also research the teachers at these sanghas. Teachers are addressed as **sensei** when they've been granted authority to teach, and **roshi** (Zen Master) when they've been recognized as having attained a deep level of realization. Your teacher—sensei or roshi—should have been granted teaching authority through an authentic Zen lineage. A Zen lineage is an unbroken line of transmission of teaching authority passed down generation by generation going back to antiquity. You can check the authenticity of lineages through a simple internet search. While Zen has no central certifying organization, recognized teachers are often members of organizations such as the American Zen Teachers Association, the Lay Zen Teachers Association, the Soto Zen Teachers Association, or the Soto Zen Buddhist Association.

You should also perform an internet search to be sure there's no history of scandal associated with the teacher.

A Glossary of Zen

bodhicitta—The compassionate intention to liberate all beings from suffering that serves as the motivation for Mahayana Buddhist practice.

Bodhidharma—The legendary Buddhist teacher who brought Zen from India to China in the 5th or 6th century CE.

bodhisattva—An enlightened person who is motivated by compassion to liberate all beings from suffering. Also, any Mahayana Buddhist practitioner who has aroused bodhicitta and taken bodhisattva vows.

bodhisattva vows—A set of Mahayana vows to 1) liberate all beings from suffering, 2) eliminate the mental defilements of greed, hatred, and delusion, 3) master the Dharma, and 4) become a Buddha.

Buddha—The historic originator of Buddhism, known as Siddhartha Gautama before his Enlightenment and Shakyamuni Buddha afterward. Also, anyone who achieves perfect Enlightenment. According to some beliefs, celestial Enlightened beings who symbolize different aspects of Enlightenment.

Buddhadharma—The teachings of the Buddha, often referred to more simply as just the *Dharma*.

buddha-nature—The capacity to realize Enlightenment common to all sentient beings. Also, the natural clarity of mind freed from greed, hatred, and delusion which is always potentially available to us in zazen.

daisan—A brief one-on-one meeting with a Zen sensei to discuss practice or work on a koan.

dharanis—Buddhist ritual incantations, often consisting of Sanskrit syllables, thought to create merit, bring good luck, or ward off evil, and that can be used as a focus of meditation.

divine abodes—The mental states of loving-kindness, compassion, sympathetic joy, and equanimity, also known as the *brahmaviharas*.

dokusan—A brief one-on-one meeting with a Zen roshi to discuss practice or work on a koan.

enso—A hand-drawn circle, executed in a single ink brushstroke, exemplifying the Zen qualities of naturalness, spontaneity, and simplicity.

gatha—A Buddhist verse teaching some aspect of the buddha-dharma.

jukai—The ceremony signifying acceptance of the Zen bodhisattva ethical precepts.

karma—The Buddhist law of cause-and-effect. The consequences of our thoughts and actions.

kensho—Literally, "seeing one's true nature." A sudden enlightenment experience. A direct experience of nonduality and emptiness.

kinhin—Walking meditation. When doing kinhin, one focuses on the sensations in one's feet as one walks.

koan—A cryptic phrase, question, or snippet of teacher-student dialogue that serves as a focus of meditative investigation.

Mahayana—The school of Buddhism that originated in India around the first century CE and spread throughout China, Korea, Japan, and Vietnam. "Mahayana" means "large vehicle."

mantra—A Sanskrit syllable, set of syllables, or short phrase that can be used as a focus of meditation or chanted aloud and is thought to have beneficial effects.

mindfulness—Awareness of thoughts, feelings, bodily sensations, and sense perceptions in the present moment without judgment, clinging, or avoidance.

nirvana—The enlightened state in which greed, hatred, and delusion have been permanently extinguished.

rakasu—A hand-sewn, bib-like ritual garment signifying acceptance of the Bodhisattva ethical precepts.

Rinzai—The school of Zen that emphasizes koan practice and the attainment of satori.

roshi—In American Zen, a Zen Master; in Japanese Zen, "old revered teacher." Roshis have received full Dharma transmission from another Zen Master. In Rinzai Zen, Roshis have successfully completed the Rinzai koan curriculum.

sangha—A community of Buddhist practitioners.

satori—A sudden enlightenment experience. A direct experience of nonduality and emptiness. Often used synonymously with *kensho*.

sensei—A person authorized to teach within a Zen lineage.

sesshin—An intensive multiday Zen meditation retreat.

shikantaza—"Just sitting." A form of zazen in which attention is directed to the whole of one's field of experiencing, nonjudgmentally observing mental phenomena as they arise and pass.

Soto—The school of Zen that emphasizes shikantaza and the teachings of Zen Master Dogen.

sutra—A Buddhist sacred scripture; usually a teaching of the Buddha.

teisho—A Zen talk delivered by a teacher.

Theravada—The school of Buddhism that began in India and was transmitted to Sri Lanka, Burma, Thailand, Laos, and Cambodia. "Theravada" means "doctrine of the elders."

Vajrayana—The school of Mahayana Buddhism that includes Indian tantric (esoteric) teachings and is identified with the Buddhism of Tibet, Nepal, Bhutan, Mongolia, and Siberia, as well as with Japanese Shingon Buddhism. "Vajrayana" means "diamond vehicle."

zafu—A round meditation cushion, usually stuffed with kapok or buckwheat hulls.

zabuton—A rectangular meditation mat on which a zafu is placed.

zazen—Seated Zen meditation practice. Zazen includes breath-focused meditation, shikantaza, and koan meditation.

zazenkai—An all-day or half-day meditation retreat.

Zen—A school of Mahayana Buddhism, originating in China, Korea, Japan, and Vietnam, that stresses seated meditation and koan practice.

Resources

Zen Books

Anderson, Tenshin Reb. *Being Upright: Zen Meditation and the Bodhisattva Precepts*. Boston: Shambhala, 2016.

A good introduction to the Zen bodhisattva precepts written by a senior Zen teacher at the San Francisco Zen Center.

Beck, Charlotte Joko. *Everyday Zen: Love and Work*. San Francisco: Harper and Row, 1989.

This collection of easy-to-understand essays focuses on how Zen applies to everyday life. Charlotte Joko Beck was the head teacher of the Zen Center of San Diego and co-founder of the Ordinary Mind School of Zen.

Beck, Charlotte Joko. *Nothing Special: Living Zen*. San Francisco: Harper, 1993.

Another collection of accessible essays by the co-founder of the Ordinary Mind School of Zen.

Ford, James Ishmael. *If You're Lucky Your Heart Will Break: Field Notes from a Zen Life*. Boston: Wisdom, 2012.

A relatable account of the wisdom gained through a life of Zen practice, written by a co-founder of the Boundless Way School of Zen.

Hanh, Thich Nhat. *The Miracle of Mindfulness*. Boston: Beacon Press, 1999.

A clearly written introduction to mindfulness by the universally beloved Vietnamese Zen Master.

Kapleau, Phillip. *The Three Pillars of Zen: Teaching, Practice, and Enlightenment*. New York: Anchor, 2000.

A classic introduction to Zen practice by the founder of the Rochester Zen Center. Kapleau Roshi taught within the Sambo Kyodan Zen tradition, which blends elements of Rinzai and Soto Zen.

Okumura, Shohaku. *Living by Vow: A Practical Introduction to Eight Essential Zen Chants and Texts*. Boston: Wisdom, 2012.

A wise and clear introduction to classic Zen chants and texts by the abbot of the Sanshin Zen Community in Bloomington, Indiana. Roshi Okumura is also the former Director of the Soto Zen Buddhism International Center, the official U.S. administrative office of the Soto school of Japan.

Suzuki, Shunryu. *Zen Mind, Beginner's Mind*. Boston: Shambhala, 2011.

The classic edited collection of Dharma talks by the founder of the San Francisco Zen Center and the teacher most responsible for making Soto Zen practice accessible to English-speaking practitioners. These talks are simple, yet profound. While a beginner can glean something from them, even experienced practitioners will at times find it difficult to plumb their depths. Year after year, American Zen practitioners rate this as the single best Zen book.

Uchiyama, Kosho. *Opening the Hand of Thought: Foundations of Zen Buddhist Practice*. Boston: Wisdom, 2004.

A classic text that gets at the very heart of Zen practice by the late Abbot of Antiji Temple near Kyoto, Japan.

Watts, Alan. *The Way of Zen*. New York: Vintage, 1999.

A classic book that played a major role in introducing the English-speaking world to Zen. Watts was a brilliant but idiosyncratic figure who never devoted himself seriously to Zen practice. As a writer, however, he is second to none. He has an unparalleled ability to explain profound ideas in easy to grasp language.

Zen Online

The World Buddhist Directory (http://www.buddhanet.info/wbd/) contains a searchable database of local Zen Buddhist practice groups and centers located throughout the world.

The Zensite (http://www.thezensite.com) maintains a listing of Zen centers, as well as a compendium of English-language translations of sutras, koans, teishos, essays, and other Zen resources.

References

Buswell, Robert, and Donald Lopez. *The Princeton Dictionary of Buddhism*. Princeton, NJ: Princeton University Press, 2014.

Gethin, Rupert. *The Foundations of Buddhism*. Oxford, UK: Oxford University Press, 1998.

Segall, Seth. *Buddhism and Human Flourishing*. New York: Palgrave Macmillan, 2020.

Shibayama, Zenkei. *The Gateless Barrier: Zen Comments on the Mumonkon*. Boston: Shambhala, 2000.

Skilton, Andrew. *A Concise History of Buddhism*. Birmingham, UK: Windhorse Publications, 1994.

Index

Acknowledgments

It takes a village to write a book, and for that reason among others, words of appreciation are in order. First and foremost, I am deeply grateful to my wife, Susan Mirialakis, whose close reading of early drafts and many helpful suggestions significantly improved the quality of this book.

I am grateful for the wisdom and guidance of Zen teachers: Daiken Nelson Sensei, Robert Jinsen Kennedy Roshi, Grover Genro Gaunt Roshi, Robert Chodo Campbell Sensei, Koshin Ellison Paley Sensei, Michael Koryu Holleran Sensei, Paul Schubert Sensei, Carl Chimon Viggiani Sensei, and Russ Kaishin Michel Sensei. I am also grateful for meditation teachers: Toni Packer, Larry Rosenberg, Joseph Goldstein, Sharon Salzberg, Tsoknyi Rinpoche, Myoshin Kelley, Ruth Denison, Ferris Urbanowski, and Jon Kabat-Zinn. They have all been my teachers, but they are not responsible for the content of the book. Any mistakes I may have inadvertently made in conveying the Zen tradition are strictly my own.

Finally, I wish to thank Callisto Media, more specifically, Joe Cho, Shannon Criss, and Laurie White for inviting me to write this book and guiding me through the publication process.

About the Author

Seth Zuihō Segall, Ph.D. is a Zen priest and retired clinical psychologist who served for nearly three decades on the clinical faculty of the Yale School of Medicine. He also taught on the faculties of Southeast Missouri State University, Southern Illinois University at Carbondale, and the State University of New York at Purchase. He is a former director of psychology at Waterbury Hospital, and a former president of the New England Society for the Study of Trauma and Dissociation.

Dr. Segall has been a practicing Buddhist for twenty-five years. He was ordained in the White Plum Zen lineage under the preceptorship of Daiken Nelson Sensei.

Dr. Segall's publications include *Encountering Buddhism: Western Psychology and Buddhist Teachings* (SUNY Press, 2003) and *Buddhism and Human Flourishing: A Modern Western Perspective* (Palgrave Macmillan, 2020). He is the science writer for the *Mindfulness Research Monthly* and a chaplain associate at White Plains Hospital. His blog, *The Existential Buddhist* (www.existentialbuddhist.com), provides insights on Buddhist philosophy, practice, ethics, history, art, and social engagement.